BOGAN TO LIAR

Bogan to Liar

JADE DOE

Copyright © 2025 by Jade Doe
All rights reserved. No part of this book may be reproduced in any manner whatsoever without written permission except in the case of brief quotations embodied in critical articles and reviews.
First Printing, 2025

CONTENTS

1	The House with the Pool	1
2	Origin Story	5
3	Bongs and Bureaucracy	10
4	Houses	16
5	Back to the Bloodline	23
6	The Sleepover	31
7	Awesome on Paper	38
8	History Repeating	47
9	Up North	54
10	The Good Aunty	61
11	Back to Mum	68
12	Freefall	76
13	The Chaos Twin	84
14	The First Big Lie	91

15	The Abuse Without Bruises	98
16	The Reinvention	105
17	Mr Three	112
18	The Daughter Who Made It	119
19	Still Lying	125

| 1 |

The House with the Pool

It's 6am and I'm standing in my kitchen waiting for the coffee machine to do its thing. The bench is stone. The appliances are matte black, because that's what people with taste choose apparently. Through the window I can see the pool - heated, salt water, skimmer working quietly in the half-light. The lawn is neat, edged last weekend by a guy I pay to make it look like I have my life together.

I do not have my life together.

I'm a liar.

Not the fun kind who spins yarns at dinner parties or embellishes fish stories. I'm the other kind. The kind who built an entire life on a foundation of bullshit so elaborate that I sometimes forget which parts are real.

Every morning I stand in this kitchen - four bedrooms, ducted air, a mortgage that suggests I'm a safe bet - and I think: is today the day? Is this the morning someone connects the dots? Googles the school I said I went to and finds no record? Mentions my name to someone from the old suburb and watches their face twist in confusion?

The house of cards doesn't fall all at once. That's not how it works. It wobbles. A question you weren't expecting. A colleague who grew up "near where you did" and wants to compare notes. A family event you can't attend because your family doesn't know this version of you exists - and the version they know isn't someone you'd introduce to polite company.

2 - JADE DOE

In an hour I'll put on clothes that cost more than my grandmother's weekly pension. I'll drive a car that doesn't have rust eating through the wheel arches. I'll walk into an office where people respect me, ask my opinion, assume I'm one of them. I'll use words I taught myself from books and meetings and listening very carefully to how other people speak. I'll laugh at jokes about bogans - those trashy people from those trashy suburbs - and no one will know they're laughing about me.

Then I'll come home to this beautiful, empty house where I have no friends, no family photos on display, and no one who knows the truth.

I broke the cycle. That's what they call it, isn't it? The cycle of poverty, abuse, addiction, bad choices passed down like heirlooms nobody asked for. I broke it. My daughter went to university. First in our family. She studies psychology now, probably trying to work out what went wrong with the rest of us.

But here's what the inspirational stories don't tell you: you can break the cycle and still be a complete mess. You can escape the caravan park and land in a house with a pool and still be paying off debt you accumulated when you didn't know that money was something you could run out of. You can build a respected career and have zero friends because friends ask questions and questions unravel lies.

I broke the cycle, but I didn't do it with grace. I did it with duct tape and denial and a fabricated backstory about a strict religious upbringing in a suburb I've driven through maybe twice. I did it by listening carefully, copying relentlessly, and erasing myself so completely that some days I catch my reflection and wonder who the hell she is.

You want to know where I actually grew up? Caravan parks. Housing commission. The kind of streets that smell like dog shit on hot days. My mother was fifteen when she had me. My father could be anyone - literally anyone - and I've never done the DNA test because I'm scared he'll turn out to be a cousin or a deadbeat or dead, and I'm not sure which would be worse.

I was in foster care before I could form permanent memories. I was back with family before the system could save me. I was shuffled between my grandmother and my mother like a problem neither of them wanted to solve, and the official child services file on me is thick enough to prop open a door.

I've read that file. Freedom of Information request when I turned eighteen. Clinical language describing things that still wake me up at night. "House likely messy." "Child expressed desire to be rehomed." "Unexplained absences from school." They documented everything. They did nothing.

So yes. I'm a liar.

I lie about where I'm from. I lie about who my family is. I lie about why I can't come to your barbecue, your wedding, your casual Friday drinks where someone might ask a follow-up question I can't answer. I lie about why there are no photos of my childhood in this immaculate house. I lie about why I don't talk about my parents. I lie about why I'm always, always alone.

I've been lying for fifteen years and I've gotten good at it. Good enough that I've dated men for years who never met a single member of my family. Good enough that I've held senior positions in companies that would have quietly shuffled my resume to the bottom of the pile if they knew the truth.

This book is the only place the truth exists.

I'm writing it under a pen name because I'm still living the lie. I'm not ready to burn it all down. Maybe I never will be. Maybe I'll die in this nice house with the pool, and someone will clean out my things and find nothing that connects me to the girl in the caravan park, and that will be the final successful lie.

But I wanted to tell someone. I wanted it written down somewhere, even if "somewhere" is a book bought by strangers who'll never know my real name.

So here's the deal: you're getting the true story. The whole ugly, absurd, sometimes darkly funny disaster of how I got from there to here. You'll meet Mum, who kicked me out at fifteen because I reminded her of something she didn't want to see. You'll meet Nan, who the system kept returning me to like a defective product. You'll meet the aunties - one who tried to save me and one who was just as broken as I was. You'll meet the men I chose badly and the children I raised imperfectly and the version of myself I invented to survive.

Some of you will read this and recognise something. A detail. A timeline. A story that sounds familiar. Some of you might even figure out who I am.

And some of you might be reading this thinking: I'm a liar too.

Maybe you grew up somewhere you don't talk about. Maybe your family is a mess you've tidied away. Maybe you've learned to code-switch so well that nobody at work would ever guess where you came from. Maybe you're sitting in your own nice house, with your own quiet dread, wondering when your cards will fall.

If that's you - I see you. This book is for you too.

And if you figure out who I am, I'm asking you for one thing: let me live my lie.

It's all I have. It's the only thing standing between me and a past that would swallow me whole. I built this life out of nothing but audacity and desperation, and I'm not ready to watch it collapse. Maybe that makes me a coward. Maybe it makes me a fraud. But I've been called worse by people who were supposed to love me, so I can live with it.

I broke the cycle.

I just broke myself a little bit in the process.

| 2 |

Origin Story

Every good story has an origin. Superman had Krypton. Batman had the alley. I had a caravan park in Queensland and a fourteen-year-old girl who made choices that would ripple through decades.

My mother was fourteen when she got pregnant with me.

Let that sink in for a moment. Fourteen. In some states, she wouldn't have been old enough to babysit. She was a year away from being allowed to get a learner's permit. She was, by any legal or moral definition, a child. And she was living in a caravan park, sleeping with a man - and I use that term loosely, because anyone sleeping with a fourteen-year-old is not a man but something else entirely - possibly for money.

I say "possibly" because the family stories are vague on this point. Nobody comes out and says "your mother was a teenage prostitute," but nobody denies it either. It's one of those things that gets talked around, hinted at, left to float in the space between words. What I know for certain is this: my mother was fourteen, she was in a caravan with a male who was decidedly not fourteen, and my grandmother found them.

The way Nan tells it - and Nan tells it with a certain grim satisfaction, like she's the hero of this particular story - she walked into that caravan and found her daughter in the act. With a grown man. In the middle of the day. In a caravan park where everyone knew everyone and nobody said a goddamn thing.

Nan dragged her out. Physically. By whatever part of her she could grab. There was yelling - Nan was always good at yelling - and threats, and the kind of scene that in a normal neighbourhood would have brought police. But this wasn't a normal neighbourhood. This was a caravan park in Queensland in the early eighties, where people minded their own business even when their business should have been calling the cops.

The man left the next day. Packed up and vanished before anyone could ask questions like "what's your name" or "how old are you" or "do you understand that what you did is a crime." He was gone. A ghost. A sperm donor with a head start.

And that, as far as anyone knows, is my father.

I've never met him. I don't know his name. I don't know if he's alive or dead, in prison or in parliament, a tradesman or a teacher or a professional predator who moved from caravan park to caravan park finding vulnerable girls. I don't know if I have his eyes, his nose, his laugh. I don't know if he ever thought about the girl he left behind or the baby that might have resulted from his afternoon in that caravan.

I could find out. DNA testing exists now. You spit in a tube, send it off, and a few weeks later you get a list of genetic relatives and a pie chart telling you what percentage Irish or Italian or Indigenous you are. People do it all the time. They find long-lost siblings, biological parents, family they never knew existed. Heartwarming reunions. Closure.

I haven't done it.

I tell myself it's because I don't care. I've made it this far without a father; I don't need one now. But that's a lie - one of many - and if this book is about anything, it's about telling the truth even when it's uncomfortable.

The truth is: I'm scared.

I'm scared that I'll spit in that tube and find out my father is a cousin. That the caravan park was small and everyone was someone's relative and my mother's mystery man was actually not so mysterious to the family tree. Inbreeding happens in insular communities. It's not talked about, but it happens.

I'm scared that I'll find him and he'll be a drunk. A deadbeat. Someone still living in a caravan park, still making bad choices, still exactly the kind of person I've spent fifteen years pretending I'm not connected to. Meeting him would be like meeting a ghost of a future I narrowly avoided.

I'm scared that I'll find him and he'll be dead. That I'll have waited too long, asked too late, and the answers will be buried with him.

And I'm scared that I'll find him and he'll be... fine. Normal. A guy who made a terrible choice at twenty-something and went on to have a regular life with a regular family who know nothing about the fourteen-year-old in the caravan. What would I do with that? Show up on his doorstep and say "Hi, I'm the consequence you forgot about"?

So I let sleeping dogs lie. It's a skill I've developed over the years - knowing when not to ask questions, when not to dig, when to accept the incomplete story because the complete one might be worse.

My mother, freshly fifteen, gave birth to me in a hospital that I've never visited. I don't know if Nan was there. I don't know if anyone was there, besides the nurses and doctors who were obligated to be. I was born to a child, in the legal sense - a ward of the state herself by that point, because someone somewhere had finally noticed that a pregnant fifteen-year-old living in a caravan park might need some official supervision.

After I was born, Mum moved into another caravan with her friend. Not home to Nan. Not to a group home or a shelter or anywhere with actual adults in charge. Just... another caravan. Another temporary space with thin walls and no running water and a baby that cried in the night.

I try to imagine it sometimes. Fifteen years old. A newborn. A caravan. No partner, no money, no idea what you're doing. Just you and this screaming thing that needs everything from you when you're still basically a child yourself. Did she love me? Did she resent me? Did she look at my face and try to figure out which parts came from the man in the caravan, the one who ran?

I don't know. I've never asked. Some conversations we've never had and probably never will.

What I do know is that Child Services was watching. For once, the system was paying attention. Mum was a ward of the state, which meant there was paperwork, oversight, people whose job it was to make sure she wasn't screwing this up completely.

And my grandmother was helping them.

Nan reported everything. Every mistake, every misstep, every bong left lying around the caravan where anyone - including a social worker - might see it. And there were bongs. Plural. My teenage mother, overwhelmed with a baby she wasn't equipped to raise, was coping the only way she knew how: by getting high.

I don't blame her for that. Not anymore. I've done enough reading about trauma, enough late-night Googling about teenage mothers and the outcomes for their children, to understand that she was set up to fail from the moment the test came back positive. Maybe earlier. Maybe from the moment she ended up in that caravan with that man. Maybe from whatever happened in her own childhood that made a caravan park and a stranger's attention feel like a reasonable option.

But understanding isn't the same as forgiving. And I'm not sure I've done either, if I'm honest.

Nan's reports to Child Services were thorough. She was in that caravan regularly, noting the mess, the smell, the drug paraphernalia, the state of the baby - me - in the middle of it all. She was building a case, though I don't think she would have called it that. She probably told herself she was protecting me. Maybe she was. Or maybe she was punishing her daughter for the embarrassment, the scandal, the proof that her parenting had produced a teenager who got knocked up by a stranger in a caravan park.

Either way, the result was the same. The evidence piled up. The social workers took notes. And at some point - I was three, maybe four, too young to remember - they decided that my mother wasn't capable of keeping me safe.

They took me away.

And that, in theory, should have been the beginning of a different story. The foster care story. The one where the system intervenes, removes a child from a bad situation, places them somewhere stable and loving, and gives them a chance at a normal life.

For about five minutes, that's exactly what happened.

Then they gave me back.

The thing about my origin story is that it doesn't have a hero. Batman had his parents, gunned down but righteous. Superman had Jor-El, sacrificing himself to save his son. I had a teenage mother who couldn't cope, a grandmother who used the system as a weapon, a father who evaporated before dawn, and a bureaucracy that would shuffle me back and forth for the next decade like they couldn't quite figure out where I belonged.

Spoiler: they never figured it out.

But we'll get to that.

For now, just know this: I started life as a problem. An inconvenience. A consequence of bad choices made by people too young or too reckless to understand what they were creating. Nobody planned for me. Nobody prepared for me. I arrived anyway, screaming into the Queensland heat, and the world had to figure out what to do with me.

It's still figuring it out.

So am I.

| 3 |

Bongs and Bureaucracy

I don't remember the caravan. Not really. I have impressions - the smell of canvas and mildew, the way light came through thin curtains, the feeling of being small in a cramped space - but I can't say for certain if those are real memories or things I've constructed from stories told later. The brain does that. Fills in gaps. Builds narratives from fragments.

What I know about those years comes from two sources: family stories, which are unreliable at best, and my Child Services file, which is clinical but thorough. Between them, I can piece together what my early childhood looked like.

It looked like bongs on the coffee table.

My mother, teenage and overwhelmed, had discovered that marijuana made everything feel slightly more manageable. The crying baby. The tiny caravan. The complete absence of a future she could see. A cone or two took the edge off, smoothed out the rough parts, made it possible to get through another day without completely falling apart.

I understand this now, as an adult. I don't condone it, but I understand it. When you have nothing - no money, no support, no roadmap for how to raise a child when you're barely more than a child yourself - you reach for whatever numbs the panic. For my mother, that was pot. Later it would be other things, other coping mechanisms, other ways of checking out when reality got too heavy. But in those caravan years, it was just weed.

The problem was that she wasn't subtle about it.

Bongs left out where anyone could see them. The smell of smoke clinging to the curtains, to my clothes, to everything. Red eyes and slow reactions when the social workers came to check on the teenage ward of the state and her infant daughter. My mother might as well have hung a sign on the caravan door: "UNFIT PARENT - PLEASE INVESTIGATE."

And investigate they did. Child Services was already watching - Mum's status as a ward meant there was built-in oversight - but they might have been content with occasional check-ins if not for Nan.

Nan was a regular visitor to that caravan. Helping, she would have said. Keeping an eye on things. Making sure her granddaughter - me - was being looked after. And maybe some of that was true. Maybe she did change nappies and wash bottles and do the things that needed doing while my mother sat glassy-eyed on the couch.

But Nan was also taking notes.

Every bong. Every mess. Every moment my mother seemed checked out or incompetent or high. Nan catalogued it all and reported back to Child Services with the dedication of someone building a legal case. Which, in retrospect, is exactly what she was doing.

I've thought a lot about Nan's motivations. Was she genuinely worried about me? Did she truly believe I was in danger and needed to be removed? Or was there something else going on - something more practical, more transactional?

Here's what I've come to believe: Nan wanted me. But not necessarily because she loved me or felt some grandmotherly urge to protect me. Nan wanted me because I came with a payment.

In Australia, when you take on the care of a child - especially a child who's been removed from their parents, especially a child with a file at Child Services - you receive money. Carer payments. Family Tax Benefits. Various government supplements designed to help cover the cost of raising a kid who isn't biologically yours.

It's not a fortune. It's not enough to get rich on. But for someone like Nan - someone who bounced between caravan parks and rental houses, who worked odd jobs and never quite had enough, who would later gamble away sixty thousand dollars because money management wasn't exactly her strength - those payments represented something significant. Stability, maybe. Or at least the illusion of it.

I'm not saying Nan didn't care about me. I'm not saying it was purely mercenary. But I am saying that every time she reported my mother's failings to Child Services, every piece of evidence she gathered, every step that brought me closer to being removed - she knew what was waiting at the end. She knew that if Mum lost custody, the next logical placement would be family. And family meant Nan. And Nan meant payments.

Follow the money, they say. In my family, the money trail leads straight through my childhood.

The reports piled up. Mum wasn't getting better - if anything, she was getting worse. The bongs multiplied. The caravan got messier. The teenage mother showed no signs of developing the skills or stability needed to raise a child. Child Services visited and took notes and expressed concerns and did all the bureaucratic things that bureaucracies do when they're watching a slow-motion disaster.

And then, when I was somewhere between three and four years old, they finally acted.

I don't remember the day they took me. I don't know if I cried, if I reached for my mother, if I understood what was happening. I was too young. The memory doesn't exist, or if it does, it's buried so deep I can't access it.

What I know is this: one day I was in a caravan with a mother who was barely coping, and the next day I was somewhere else. Officially removed. Placed into foster care. A ward of the state myself now, just like my mother had been.

The system had finally done its job. Months - years - of documentation and concern and hand-wringing had resulted in action. I was out. Safe. Given a chance at something different.

And for a little while, that's exactly what I got.

But before we get to the foster homes - the good part, the brief window where I glimpsed what normal looked like - I want to stay with this moment a bit longer. The taking. The removal. The day the government decided my mother wasn't capable of raising me.

Because here's the thing: they were right. She wasn't capable. The bongs, the mess, the neglect - it was all real. The reports weren't fabricated. My mother was failing, and I was the one paying the price.

But they were also late. Years late. They'd watched and documented and expressed concern while I lived in that caravan breathing secondhand smoke and learning that chaos was normal. They'd given my teenage mother chance after chance to get her shit together, knowing she had no support, no skills, no realistic path to improvement.

And when they finally did act, where did they initially look to place me? Family. Specifically, the family member who'd been reporting all the problems. Nan. The woman who'd built the case against her own daughter.

The system's logic was this: children should be with family when possible. Blood matters. Kinship placements are preferable to stranger care. It sounds reasonable on paper. In practice, it meant that the same family that produced a teenage mother in a caravan - the same family that failed to protect her, that let her end up pregnant at fourteen, that had its own histories and dysfunctions and cycles of disaster - was considered the ideal place to send the child removed from that situation.

It's like taking a plant out of toxic soil and replanting it in the same garden, just a few feet over.

But I'm getting ahead of myself. Before Nan got her hands on me - and her payments - there was foster care. There were the houses. And for the first time in my short life, I experienced something that I didn't have words for yet but would spend the next thirty years chasing.

Stability.

Years later, when I was eighteen and angry and desperate to understand why my life had gone the way it had, I submitted a Freedom of Information request for my Child Services file.

The file arrived in a thick envelope. Pages and pages of reports, case notes, assessments, meeting minutes. My entire childhood reduced to bureaucratic language and checkbox evaluations. "Child appears healthy." "Mother cooperative but concerns remain." "Grandmother reports ongoing drug use in the home."

There it was in black and white. Nan's reports. Dated and documented. A paper trail showing exactly how involved she'd been in building the case against Mum.

And scattered through those pages, in the dry language of government workers just doing their jobs, was the outline of my early life. The caravan. The concerns. The removal. The placement decisions and the reasoning behind them.

One phrase stuck with me. I don't remember the exact context - which report, which social worker - but the words lodged in my brain like a splinter.

"Grandmother has expressed willingness to assume care."

Willingness. Such a clean word. It suggests generosity, sacrifice, stepping up when others have stepped back. It doesn't capture the complexity - the history, the motivations, the money that would change hands.

Nan was willing to assume care.

Nan was willing to receive the payments that came with that care.

Nan was willing to raise the granddaughter her daughter couldn't manage, in the same environment that had produced that daughter in the first place.

The system noted her willingness and called it a solution.

But first, the detour. The foster homes. The glimpse behind the curtain at how other people lived.

I was about to learn that dinner could happen at a table. That toilets could be inside houses. That families could go to beaches and have picnics and speak to each other without yelling.

I was about to learn, at three or four years old, that everything I knew was wrong.

It would be the most disorienting, wonderful, heartbreaking experience of my early childhood.

And then they'd send me back.

| 4 |

Houses

The first foster home had a doorbell.

I know that sounds like a strange detail to lead with. Of all the things that were different about that house - and everything was different - the doorbell shouldn't have been the thing that stuck. But I remember standing at the front door, small and confused and clutching whatever belongings I'd arrived with, and hearing this musical chime from inside. Like the house was announcing me. Like arrival was an event worth marking.

Caravans don't have doorbells. You knock on the flimsy door or you just walk in or you yell from outside until someone acknowledges you. There's no ceremony to it. No pleasant chime saying "someone's here." You just appear, and people deal with it.

But this house - this actual house, with walls that didn't shake when you leaned on them and a roof that didn't echo when it rained - this house had a doorbell. And carpet. And a hallway. And rooms. Plural. Rooms that had specific purposes: this one for sleeping, this one for eating, this one for sitting. The concept of having enough space that you could dedicate entire rooms to single activities was foreign to me. In a caravan, everything happens everywhere. You sleep where you eat where you sit where you exist, all in the same cramped space.

I was scared for about five minutes.

I remember that fear - the uncertainty of being somewhere new, with people I didn't know, in a space I didn't understand. Everything was big and clean and quiet. Where was the noise? Where was the yelling? Where was the chaos that I'd learned to navigate?

But kids are adaptable. Especially kids who've already learned that their environment can change without warning. You either fall apart or you adjust. I adjusted.

And then I thought: this is cool.

The first placement was temporary. Emergency care, they call it. A holding pattern while the system figured out what to do with me long-term. The family was well-off - not rich, probably, but they seemed rich to me. They had things. Furniture that matched. Appliances that worked. Food in the fridge that wasn't expired or scavenged or someone else's leftovers.

They had a toilet inside the house.

I need you to understand what this meant to me. In the caravan, the toilet situation was... complicated. Shared amenities. Blocks you had to walk to. The smell of communal bathrooms that were cleaned on someone else's schedule, if they were cleaned at all. The nighttime calculation of whether you really needed to go badly enough to leave the caravan in the dark.

But this house had a toilet. Inside. Down the hallway. You just... went. Whenever you needed to. In your own home. Private. Clean. With toilet paper that was always there because someone made sure it was always there.

I know this sounds ridiculous. I know that for most people reading this, an indoor toilet is so baseline, so assumed, that mentioning it seems almost absurd. Of course there's a toilet inside. Where else would it be?

But that's exactly my point. The things you take for granted - the things that are so fundamental to your existence that you don't even register them as privileges - those are the things that blew my three-year-old mind. Indoor plumbing. Carpet under my feet. A bed that was just mine, that I didn't share with anyone, in a room that had walls and a door that closed.

It was like visiting another planet. A planet where everything was soft and clean and quiet.

We ate dinner at a table.

This is another one of those details that will sound unremarkable to most people. Dinner at a table. Where else would you eat dinner?

Anywhere. Everywhere. On the couch, if there was a couch. On the floor. Standing up. In front of whatever passed for a television. Out of containers, out of packets, out of your hands. Dinner, in my experience, was not an event. It was just fuel, consumed whenever and wherever it became available.

But in this foster home, dinner was a thing that happened. At a specific time. At a table with chairs around it. With plates - actual plates, not paper or plastic - and utensils and food that someone had cooked. Cooked. In a kitchen. On purpose.

The family sat down together. They talked. Asked about each other's days. Passed dishes around. Said please and thank you. It was choreographed in a way that suggested they did this every single day, that it wasn't a performance for my benefit, that this was just... how they lived.

I didn't know how to act. I remember that feeling of being on the outside of something, watching a ritual I didn't understand, trying to figure out the rules so I wouldn't do it wrong. Where do I sit? When do I start eating? Am I supposed to talk? What do I say?

They were patient with me. Kind. They explained things without making me feel stupid for not knowing. "We wait until everyone's served." "You can use your fork like this." "Would you like some more?"

Would you like some more.

Four words that contained a universe of difference. In the caravan, you ate what was there, if anything was there. You didn't ask for more because more wasn't a concept. There was what there was, and when it was gone, it was gone.

But here, there was more. And someone was offering it. Someone had made enough that there could be seconds, that a small child could want more and receive it, that abundance was normal.

I think that was the moment I realised something was very wrong with my life before this. Not in an articulate way - I was four, too young for that kind of analysis. But somewhere in my brain, a comparison was being made. This house versus that caravan. This family versus mine. This dinner versus whatever I'd been eating before.

The conclusion was wordless but clear: this was better.

They took me to the beach.

We got in a car - their car, clean and functional and not making any alarming sounds - and drove to the ocean. They had towels, proper beach towels, big and colourful. They had sunscreen that they put on me, carefully, so I wouldn't burn. They had an esky with drinks and snacks. They had thought about this outing, planned for it, prepared everything I might need.

I don't know if I'd been to a beach before that day. If I had, I don't remember it. What I remember is this trip, with these strangers who were taking care of me, standing on sand and looking at water that went on forever.

We had a picnic. Sandwiches cut into triangles. Fruit in containers. Little treats wrapped in plastic. A whole meal, transported to the beach, eaten on a blanket while the waves made their noise. It was the most extravagant thing I'd ever experienced.

A picnic at the beach. A Tuesday afternoon. Nothing special to them, probably. Just something families did. But I remember it like it was a birthday and Christmas and every good thing combined.

The second foster placement was longer. A woman - I'll call her Mrs. Second, which sounds ridiculous but this is what we're doing with names - who took in kids who needed somewhere to be. She wasn't wealthy like the first family. Her house was smaller, more modest. But it was still a house. Still had the indoor toilet. Still had the dinner table.

And she was lovely.

I don't use that word often. Lovely. It feels old-fashioned, soft, the kind of word that gets used in greeting cards. But it's the right word for her. She was warm without being overwhelming. Present without being smothering. She took care of me in a way that felt natural, like this was just what people did, like looking after a small child who wasn't yours was no big deal.

She made me feel normal. Not like a case file. Not like a problem that needed managing. Just like a kid who lived in her house and needed feeding and bathing and bedtime stories.

I stayed with her for - actually, I'm not sure how long. Months, probably. Long enough that it started to feel like home. Long enough that I learned the rhythms of her household, the rules, the expectations. Long enough that I started to relax into it, to trust that this might be my life now.

That was my mistake, of course. Trusting. Relaxing. Thinking that good things might last.

Twenty years later, I tracked her down.

I was in my twenties, trying to make sense of my life, and I remembered her. The lovely woman who'd taken care of me when I was small. I didn't have much to go on - fragments of memory, a vague sense of the suburb, the knowledge that she'd existed and been kind.

But I found her. The details of how aren't important. What matters is that I showed up at her door, an adult now, and I said thank you.

She remembered me. That's the part that still makes me cry if I think about it too long. She'd had dozens of foster kids over the years, maybe hundreds. I was one small child among many, a brief placement in a long career of caring for other people's disasters. But she remembered me.

We talked. About then, about now, about what had happened in between. I told her some of my story - not all of it, not the worst parts, but enough. She listened the way she'd probably listened to a thousand kids with a thousand terrible stories.

And I thanked her. For the house. For the meals. For treating me like I mattered. For being the first person to show me that life could be different.

She said she wished she could have kept me.

The system doesn't work like that, of course. Foster care isn't adoption. Emergency placements aren't permanent. There are rules and processes and hierarchies of preferred outcomes. Family reunification is the goal, always. Keep kids with their blood relatives when possible. Kinship placements over stranger care.

She wanted to keep me, but the system wanted me with family.

And family meant Nan.

I don't know exactly how long I was in foster care total. The file probably says, but the numbers blur together. What I know is that it was long enough to show me another way of living, and short enough that I couldn't hold onto it.

The system did what the system does. It found a "family placement." It noted that my grandmother had expressed willingness to assume care. It checked its boxes and followed its processes and decided that blood was more important than stability, that genetic connection outweighed the clean house and the dinner table and the lovely woman who'd wanted to keep me.

I was returned. Like a library book. Like a borrowed item that was due back. My brief vacation in normalcy was over, and I was going back to where I came from.

Back to the caravan. Back to Nan. Back to thin walls and shared toilets and chaos.

The houses were over.

I wouldn't live in a real house again for years.

Sometimes I think about the doorbell. That musical chime announcing my arrival at the first foster home. The sound of entering somewhere you might belong.

I don't remember a sound for leaving. No chime. No ceremony. Just a social worker and a car and a drive to wherever came next.

That's how it works when you're a kid in the system. People make decisions about your life in meetings you don't attend. You find out what's happening when it happens. You adjust, because what else can you do?

I'd gotten good at adjusting. Too good, maybe. The skill that helped me survive foster care - the ability to quickly read new environments and figure out how to fit in - would become the same skill I'd use later to reinvent myself entirely.

Adaptation was my superpower.

It was also, I would learn, a way of losing yourself entirely.

But that realisation was decades away. For now, I was just a small kid leaving a house with an indoor toilet, heading to whatever came next, carrying memories of dinner tables and beach picnics that would haunt me for the rest of my life.

Normal existed. I'd seen it. I'd tasted it.

And now it was gone.

| 5 |

Back to the Bloodline

The caravan was smaller than I remembered.

Or maybe I was bigger. Maybe the foster homes had recalibrated my sense of space, so that returning to Nan's caravan felt like climbing into a shoebox. Either way, it was a shock. The thin walls. The mildew smell. The way everything was crammed together - kitchen, bedroom, living room, all occupying the same few square metres.

And Nan, of course. Large and loud in a space that couldn't contain her.

I was back. The system had done its job - found a family placement, checked its boxes, returned me to my bloodline like that was some kind of solution. Never mind that this bloodline had produced a teenage mother who couldn't cope. Never mind that the caravan park was the same environment I'd been removed from, just with a different adult in charge. Family was family. Blood was blood. The paperwork was complete.

My Aunty was there too - the youngest of Nan's three daughters, still living at home. She was about twelve when I arrived, which meant she was thrilled to suddenly have a four-year-old roommate. And by thrilled, I mean horrified. I was not cool. I was a small, needy interruption to her teenage life, a reminder that our family couldn't get its shit together, a literal child that she now had to share her space with.

We shared a room. In a caravan, "room" is a generous term - it was more like a sectioned-off corner with a curtain for the illusion of privacy. She had her things on one side, I had whatever I'd arrived with on the other, and between us was a silent wall of resentment that no curtain could hide.

I don't blame her for that resentment. Not now, anyway. She was a kid too, stuck in the same situation I was, just a few years further along. She hadn't asked for any of this either.

But at the time, I just knew that I wasn't wanted. Again. Still. The theme of my childhood, establishing itself early.

We lived in that caravan for a couple of years. Long enough for it to become normal again. Long enough for the memories of indoor toilets and dinner tables to fade into something dreamlike, something I wasn't sure had actually happened.

Child Services, to their credit, didn't completely forget about me. They did visits. They checked in. They noted the conditions and expressed concerns and did all the bureaucratic hand-wringing that looked like action without actually changing anything.

But eventually, someone decided that a caravan wasn't an appropriate long-term placement for a child in state care. Nan was receiving payments to look after me - carer payments, family tax benefits, the various government funds that flowed her way because I existed - and those payments came with expectations. Not high expectations, mind you. But expectations nonetheless.

A house. They wanted Nan to have a house.

The waiting list for housing commission in Queensland was long. Years long, for most people. Families waited and waited, living in cars or shelters or overcrowded rentals, hoping their number would eventually come up. The system was overwhelmed, underfunded, and slow.

But Child Services had pull. They could make things happen when they wanted to. And they wanted Nan in a house.

So they pulled strings. Made calls. Bumped Nan up the queue. Suddenly, after years of nothing, there was a housing commission property available. Three bedrooms. A yard. An actual address instead of a lot number in a caravan park.

The system had intervened again. This time, instead of removing me, they were improving my conditions. Progress, right? A house was better than a caravan. Everyone agreed on that.

What no one seemed to consider was what kind of neighbourhood that house would be in.

I don't know the exact statistics, but I'd bet money that at least half the houses on that street were housing commission. Probably more. The government had a habit of concentrating its charity - building clusters of public housing in the same areas, creating entire neighbourhoods of people who had one thing in common: they couldn't afford to live anywhere else.

On paper, this made a kind of bureaucratic sense. Easier to manage. Economies of scale. All the struggling families in one place, where services could reach them efficiently.

In practice, it meant something else entirely.

It meant that every house on the street had its own disaster. Every family was fighting its own battle with poverty, addiction, mental illness, domestic violence, or some combination of all four. There was no one to look up to, no example of how things could be different, no escape from the gravity of collective dysfunction.

Bogan town. That's what people called neighbourhoods like this, though never to our faces. Just a bunch of bogans, living their bogan lives, reinforcing each other's bogan habits.

The houses looked like what they were: government-issued, minimum-viable dwellings for people the rest of society preferred not to think about. Some were maintained, sort of. Others were falling apart, with overgrown yards and broken windows and rusted-out cars in the driveways that hadn't moved in years.

The cars. God, the cars. Every second driveway had a vehicle that was more rust than metal, sitting on flat tyres or blocks, cannibalised for parts or just abandoned. They were monuments to optimism - someone had once believed that car would run again, that they'd get around to fixing it, that things would improve. The rust told a different story.

And the animals. Dogs, mostly, though there were cats and other things too. Untrained, unfenced, roaming the street in packs. They barked at all hours. They got into bins. They fought each other and sometimes people. Nobody seemed to be in charge of them, just like nobody seemed to be in charge of anything else.

On hot days, the street smelled like shit. Literally. Dog shit, mainly, baking in the Queensland sun. But also overflowing bins, and blocked drains, and whatever was rotting in those abandoned cars. The smell of neglect. The smell of giving up.

This was my new home. The system's gift to me.

The housing commission house, when you move in, comes with nothing.

I mean that literally. No curtains. No carpet - just concrete floors or bare boards. No light fixtures, in some cases. Just walls and a roof and the basic infrastructure of shelter, with everything else left for you to figure out.

We moved in from a caravan, which meant we also had nothing. No furniture. No beds. No kitchen table. No couch. We had whatever fit in the caravan and whatever we were wearing, and that was it.

Those first few weeks were rough. I remember sleeping on the floor, on blankets or towels or whatever was soft enough to cushion the concrete. I remember the echo of empty rooms, the way sound bounced around with nothing to absorb it. I remember feeling exposed - no curtains meant anyone could look in, and in a neighbourhood like ours, people looked.

Eventually, one of the big charity services came through. Lifeline, maybe, or the Salvos - I can't remember which. They had a program for exactly this situation: families moving into empty government housing with nothing to fill it. They brought furniture. Donated stuff, mismatched and worn, but furniture nonetheless. Beds. A couch. A kitchen table with chairs that didn't quite match.

We had things now. Hand-me-downs from strangers, charity cases ourselves, but things. The house started to feel less like a concrete shell and more like a place where people lived.

Nan never said thank you, as far as I remember. She took the furniture like it was owed to her, like the world had finally gotten around to providing what she deserved. That was Nan's way. Everything was someone else's responsibility - the government, the charities, the system that she'd learned to work for maximum benefit with minimum effort.

The payments kept coming. That was the important thing. Whatever else happened, the money for my care arrived on schedule.

I shared a room with my Aunty. Still.

The house had three bedrooms, which sounds like plenty. But Nan had the biggest one - obviously - and the third was... I actually don't remember what happened to the third bedroom. Storage, maybe. Or maybe one of Nan's other daughters was in and out. The housing arrangements were always fluid, people appearing and disappearing based on circumstances I didn't understand.

What I understood was that I was eight years old and sharing a room with a sixteen-year-old who wanted nothing to do with me.

She had her side. I had mine. The invisible line between us was absolute. Her stuff was not to be touched, not to be looked at, not to be acknowledged. My stuff - what little I had - stayed in my corner, out of her way.

She was at that age where everything was embarrassing, and nothing was more embarrassing than having a kid sister (technically cousin, but we were raised like siblings) cramping her style. She had friends, sometimes. Boys, eventually. Having a child in the room complicated things.

I learned to be invisible. To take up as little space as possible, physically and otherwise. To disappear into corners when she had people over, to pretend I didn't hear the things I heard, to exist without being noticed.

It was good training, actually. For later. For the life I'd eventually build, where being invisible was the whole point.

Nan didn't cook.

This seems like a small thing, but it shaped everything. The foster homes had shown me what family meals looked like - the table, the plates, the food someone had prepared with intention. I'd tasted that life. I knew it existed.

Nan's house was different. Dinner was whatever was around. Sandwiches, often. Takeaway when there was money. Cereal, regardless of time of day. The kitchen existed, technically, but it was more for storage than cooking.

The funny thing - and I mean funny in the darkest possible way - is that Nan's jobs were almost always cooking jobs. She worked in cafeterias, in canteens, in places where her job was literally to prepare food for other people. She could cook, presumably. Someone was paying her to do it.

But she never cooked for us.

I used to wonder about this. Was she too tired after cooking all day for strangers? Did she resent having to do it at home for free? Or did she just not care enough about us to make the effort?

I still don't know the answer. Maybe all three. Maybe none. Maybe cooking for your family requires something beyond skill - some investment in their wellbeing, some desire to nurture - that Nan just didn't have.

Whatever the reason, I learned early that food was a solo activity. You found what was available, you ate it, you moved on. No ceremony. No togetherness. Just fuel.

I thought about those foster home dinners sometimes. The table. The chairs. The asking if I wanted more. It felt like something I'd dreamed, or seen in a movie. Not something that had actually happened to me.

So this was my life now. A housing commission house in a housing commission neighbourhood. A room shared with a teenager who resented my existence. A grandmother who collected payments for my care but couldn't be bothered to cook me dinner. No curtains on the windows for the first few weeks. Charity furniture arranged in rooms that echoed with emptiness.

The system had helped. That was the official story. Child Services had pulled strings, gotten Nan a house, improved my living conditions. Box checked. Progress noted. Case file updated.

But standing in that house, looking out the curtainless window at the rusted cars and roaming dogs and neighbours who were just different versions of the same disaster, I didn't feel helped.

I felt relocated.

Same problems. Different postcode.

The caravan park had been temporary, even if it hadn't felt that way. Caravan parks have an transience built in - you're always sort of passing through, even when you've been there for years.

But this house felt permanent. This was where we lived now. This neighbourhood, these people, this life. The government had assigned us here, and here we would stay.

I was too young to understand concepts like "poverty trap" or "systemic disadvantage" or "concentrated social housing perpetuating cycles of dysfunction." I just knew that the street smelled bad and the other kids were rough and Nan yelled a lot and I missed the foster home with the doorbell.

But you adapt. That's what kids do. You normalise whatever your circumstances are because the alternative - recognising that your life is fundamentally different from what it should be - is too heavy to carry.

So I adapted. I learned the rules of the neighbourhood. I figured out which kids to avoid and which houses to stay away from. I developed the radar that all children in chaotic environments develop - the ability to sense when trouble is coming, when to disappear, when to be very, very quiet.

And I waited, without knowing I was waiting, for something to change.

It would. Eventually. But not for the better.

It rarely was.

| 6 |

The Sleepover

I was in grade five when I realised my life was wrong.

Not bad, exactly. Not yet. What I experienced at Nan's wasn't bad in the dramatic, reportable sense. It was just... less. Less than other people had. Less than I was supposed to have. Less than I'd glimpsed in those foster homes and then lost. It was neglect dressed up as normal. Yelling instead of talking. Absence instead of presence. The slow erosion of a childhood rather than any single catastrophic event.

But I didn't have the framework to understand that yet. When you're a kid, your life is just your life. You assume everyone's experience is roughly similar, that the way you live is the way people live, that normal is whatever happens inside your own four walls.

The sleepover changed that.

Her name doesn't matter. Let's call her Sarah, because I need to call her something. She was a girl from school - not my best friend, but friendly enough that when she invited a few girls over for a sleepover, I was included.

I'd never been to a sleepover before. The concept was exciting in an abstract way: staying up late, eating snacks, whatever it was that girls did at these things. I'd seen sleepovers in movies. They looked fun. Normal. The kind of thing normal kids did.

Nan didn't care either way. One less kid to deal with for a night. She barely looked up when I told her about the invitation, just grunted something that I interpreted as permission. I packed a bag

- what did you even bring to a sleepover? I had no idea - and got dropped off at Sarah's house after school.

The house was in a different suburb. Not far, geographically. Maybe fifteen minutes by car. But it might as well have been another country.

The first thing I noticed was the garden. Neat. Maintained. Flowers in beds, lawn mowed, edges trimmed. No rusted cars. No roaming dogs. No overflowing bins or broken fences or any of the markers I'd learned to associate with "neighbourhood."

The house itself was... normal. That's the only word for it. A normal house in a normal street where normal people lived. It wasn't a mansion. It wasn't flashy or fancy or trying to be something it wasn't. It was just a house where someone had bothered. Where effort had been made. Where things were looked after.

I didn't have words for this yet. I just knew it felt different. The air felt different. Lighter, somehow.

Sarah's mum answered the door. She was smiling. Genuinely smiling, not the tight grimace adults sometimes wore when they had to deal with children. She welcomed me in, asked if I'd had a good day at school, offered me a drink. Small talk. Hospitality. The rituals of normal human interaction that I'd seen but never quite learned.

I said yes to the drink because I didn't know what else to say. She gave me a glass - a real glass, not plastic - of juice. Fresh juice, not cordial. I held it like it was precious, which, to me, it was.

Sarah's room was upstairs. Her own room. Just hers.

I need to pause here because I'm not sure I can convey what this meant to me. I was ten years old and I had never, in my entire life, had a room of my own. I'd shared with Mum in various caravans. I'd shared with my Aunty, who hated it. I'd slept in common areas and on floors and in whatever space was available. The concept of a room - a whole room, with a door that closed - that belonged to just one person, just one child, was almost incomprehensible.

And it was decorated.

Not just furnished. Decorated. With intention. There was a colour scheme - purple, I think, or maybe pink. The bedspread matched the curtains. There were posters on the walls, arranged thoughtfully. There were shelves with books and trinkets and the accumulated treasures of a childhood that had been allowed to accumulate. There was a desk for homework. A mirror with photos tucked into the frame. Fairy lights strung around the window.

It was a room that said: a person lives here, and that person matters.

My corner of the room I shared with my Aunty had none of this. I had a bed. I had a small pile of belongings that I kept contained, out of her way. The walls were bare because decoration wasn't something that occurred to anyone. The room said nothing about me because I wasn't supposed to take up space.

I stood in Sarah's doorway and felt something shift inside me. A crack forming. A question taking shape that I wouldn't be able to unask.

The other girls arrived. We did sleepover things - talking, giggling, whatever ten-year-old girls did in the nineties. I participated, sort of. I laughed when they laughed. I agreed with whatever they agreed with. But part of me was somewhere else, cataloguing. Noticing.

The house had things. So many things. A TV in the living room - a big one, not the tiny portable that Nan sometimes had. A couch that matched other furniture. Bookshelves with books. Photos on the walls - family photos, framed and displayed, evidence of holidays and celebrations and moments worth remembering.

We had almost no photos at Nan's. I don't know if that was poverty or indifference or both. But the absence was there, now that I was looking at the presence.

Sarah's mum made dinner.

I watched her do it. She moved around the kitchen with ease, pulling things from cupboards and the fridge, chopping and stirring and checking on pots. It wasn't a production. It wasn't stressful. It was just... what she did. Part of the routine. A mother making dinner for her daughter and her daughter's friends.

She made enough for everyone. She'd planned for us, anticipated our presence, bought extra food to accommodate a handful of extra children. The meal was nothing fancy - I can't even remember what it was - but it was hot and homemade and served on plates that matched.

We sat at a table. All of us. Sarah's mum sat with us for a bit, asking about school, about our teachers, about whatever ten-year-olds wanted to talk about. Then she cleared the plates and said we could have dessert later, and there was dessert, planned and ready, because of course there was.

No one yelled. The whole evening, no one yelled.

I kept waiting for it. The tension that preceded the explosion. The shift in atmosphere that meant someone was about to lose their temper. I was braced for it, the way I was always braced for it, muscles tight, radar on.

It never came. People just... talked. In normal voices. And when they disagreed about something, they just... discussed it. Like disagreement was a thing that could happen without violence.

Then the grandmother arrived.

Sarah's grandmother. She came over that evening - maybe this was planned, maybe she just dropped by, I don't know. But she walked in the door with a tin of homemade biscuits and a warmth that filled the room.

She'd made them herself. The biscuits. For Sarah. For us. She'd thought about her granddaughter and her granddaughter's friends and decided to bake something sweet and bring it over. Just because.

I watched Sarah hug her grandmother. Easy. Natural. No flinching, no wariness, no calculation about what kind of mood she might be in. Just a kid hugging her grandma because that's what kids did with grandparents who loved them.

I thought about Nan. About the yelling. About the way I'd learned to read her moods and stay out of her way. About how a hug was not something that happened between us, not like that, not easy and warm and safe.

The biscuits were good. I ate two, then felt guilty for taking too much, then was offered more and didn't know how to respond.

Later that night, after we'd watched a movie and eaten too much sugar and done all the sleepover things, I found myself alone with Sarah's mum for a moment. The other girls were in the bathroom or getting changed or whatever. It was just me and this woman who'd spent her evening feeding us, looking after us, making us feel welcome.

I asked her a question. I don't know where it came from - some deep place where the crack had formed, where the comparisons were piling up, where the question had been taking shape all evening.

"How did you get all this stuff?"

I meant the house. The furniture. The decorated room. The food and the grandmother and the life that seemed so impossibly abundant compared to mine. How did you get it? Where did it come from? What's the secret that everyone else seems to know except me?

She looked at me. I remember her expression - a little surprised, maybe a little sad, like she could hear what I was really asking underneath the words.

"I worked hard," she said.

That was it. Simple. Direct. I worked hard.

I nodded like I understood. Like that explained everything. Like working hard was a thing I could go home and do and then I'd have a house like this too, a room that was just mine, a grandmother who brought biscuits.

I didn't understand, of course. I was ten.

I didn't understand that "working hard" required opportunities to work, jobs that paid enough to build something, an absence of the chaos that swallowed every dollar before it could accumulate. I didn't understand that Nan probably worked hard too, in her own way, but that her hard work went to different things - survival, addiction, the constant scramble of poverty. I didn't understand systemic disadvantage or generational trauma or any of the structural factors that made Sarah's house possible and my house inevitable.

I just heard: I worked hard. And I absorbed the corollary: if your life isn't like this, you didn't work hard enough. Your family didn't try hard enough. You deserve what you have because you haven't earned anything different.

It's a brutal lesson to learn at ten. It's also, in its own limited way, not entirely wrong. Work matters. Effort matters. The choices you make compound over time.

But it's not the whole story. It's not even most of the story. It leaves out everything - the starting points, the safety nets, the thousand invisible advantages that make hard work pay off for some people and not others.

I didn't know any of this then. I just knew that Sarah's mum had worked hard and had a nice house, and Nan hadn't worked hard enough and that's why we lived the way we lived.

It would take me decades to complicate that understanding. To see the full picture. To extend some grace to the people who'd raised me, even while holding them accountable for their choices.

At ten, I just felt shame.

I went home the next day with something new inside me. A knowledge I couldn't unknow. A comparison I couldn't unmake.

My life was different from other people's lives. Not just a little different. Fundamentally different. The gap between Sarah's house and Nan's house wasn't about decoration or furniture. It was about everything. The way people spoke to each other. The presence or absence of food. The feeling of safety versus the feeling of waiting for something to go wrong.

I'd been to the foster homes. I'd seen glimpses. But I'd been so young then, and it had been so brief, and I'd managed to convince myself that maybe I'd imagined it, or maybe everyone lived in caravans and I'd just gotten lucky for a while.

The sleepover destroyed that comfortable lie. I was old enough now to understand what I was seeing. Old enough to compare. Old enough to ask questions that didn't have good answers.

How did you get all this stuff?

I worked hard.

Okay. Okay, then. I'd work hard. I'd figure it out. I'd get myself a house with a decorated room and a grandmother who brought biscuits and a life where no one yelled.

I didn't know how yet. I didn't know the path. But I knew, walking back into Nan's housing commission house with its mismatched charity furniture and its bare walls and its smell of neglect, that I wasn't going to stay here.

I was going to work hard. And I was going to get out.

Looking back, I can see that sleepover as a turning point. Not the dramatic kind - no one died, nothing exploded, my circumstances didn't change. But something inside me shifted. The crack became a fissure. The question became a mission.

I didn't know yet that working hard wouldn't be enough. That I'd have to lie, too. That I'd have to erase where I came from, invent a new history, become someone else entirely.

But the seed was planted that night, in Sarah's purple bedroom with the matching curtains and the fairy lights.

I wanted that life.

And I understood, for the first time, that wanting wasn't enough. I'd have to take it.

Whatever it took.

| 7 |

Awesome on Paper

Child Services loved a checklist.

House? Check. Husband? Check. Other children being raised successfully? Check. Stable address, employment history, no recent incidents? Check, check, check.

My mother, at some point during my early childhood, had managed to tick all the boxes. She'd moved to Victoria with her husband - my stepfather - and they'd built what looked, from the outside, like a functional life. They had a house. Not a caravan, not a housing commission rental, but an actual house that they were buying. They had two kids together, my half-siblings, who appeared to be fed and clothed and alive. They had jobs. They had a postcode in a country town where everyone knew everyone and problems got noticed.

On paper, they looked awesome.

And so, when I was eight years old, Child Services made a decision. It was time for me to go home. Not home to Nan's housing commission house with its bare walls and charity furniture. Home to Mum. To the family I was supposed to have been part of all along.

The system had done its job. The mother who'd lost custody due to bongs and chaos had reformed herself. She was ready now. The paperwork said so.

I don't remember being asked if I wanted to go. Maybe I was. Maybe there was a meeting, a conversation, a social worker gently explaining that I'd be living with my real mum now, wouldn't that be nice? If it happened, I've blocked it out. What I remember is being put on a plane - my first plane, which should have been exciting but was mostly terrifying - and landing somewhere cold.

Queensland to Victoria. It shouldn't have felt like another country, but it did.

The cold was the first shock.

I'd spent my entire life in Queensland, where winter meant maybe wearing a jumper in the morning. Victoria was different. Victoria had actual cold - the kind that hurt your face, that made your fingers ache, that required layers of clothing I didn't own and hadn't known existed.

Mum didn't think to prepare me for this. I arrived with my Queensland wardrobe, which was completely inadequate, and spent the first few weeks shivering in borrowed jumpers that didn't fit. A small thing, maybe. But it set the tone. I was unprepared for this new life in ways that went far beyond clothing.

The town was country. Properly country. One main street, everyone knowing everyone's business, the kind of place where people waved at passing cars because they probably knew who was driving. After the housing commission neighbourhood with its anonymous dysfunction, this felt exposed. Visible. Like there was nowhere to hide.

Mum and Stepdad's house was on a quiet street. It had a yard. It had rooms - more rooms than people, which still felt luxurious to me. It had a kitchen where, miracle of miracles, my mother actually cooked.

Mum cooked dinner.

I need to sit with this for a moment, because it was so disorienting. The mother who'd raised me in a caravan full of bong smoke, who'd lost custody because she couldn't get her shit together, who existed in my memory as a cautionary tale told by Nan - that mother was now standing in a kitchen, preparing meals. For a family. Her family.

There were bedtimes. Actual bedtimes, enforced with actual consequences. There was structure - wake up at this time, school at this time, dinner at this time, bed at this time. The chaos I'd grown up with had been replaced by routine, and I didn't know what to do with it.

I should have been happy. This was what normal looked like, right? This was what I'd glimpsed at the foster homes, what I'd seen at Sarah's house during the sleepover. Structure. Meals. A mother who was present.

But something was off. I could feel it, even at seven, even without the words to describe it. The surface looked right, but underneath, the current was wrong.

I shared a room with my little sister. Half-sister, technically, but we didn't use that language. She was three, young enough that she didn't understand why this strange older girl had suddenly appeared in her house and her room.

Her room. That was the thing. It had been her room, decorated for her, filled with her things. Her toys. Her books. Her clothes in the closet, her drawings on the walls. And then I arrived, and suddenly she had to share.

She had toys. I did not.

The disparity was immediate and obvious. She had accumulated years of birthday presents, Christmas presents, random treats from parents who were present and employed and able to provide. I had whatever I'd brought from Nan's, which was essentially nothing.

I don't think anyone meant for this to be cruel. It just was. The visual reminder, every day, that she had been wanted and planned for and provided for, and I had been... elsewhere. An afterthought. A box that Child Services had finally gotten around to checking.

Mum didn't rush to fix this imbalance. Maybe money was tight. Maybe she didn't notice. Maybe, on some level, the distinction felt appropriate to her - this was her real daughter, her do-over, and I was the mistake from before that had finally caught up with her.

I'm speculating. I don't actually know what Mum thought. We never talked about it. We never talked about much of anything, really.

The pot was still there.

This was the first thing I noticed that confirmed my sense that something was wrong. Mum and Stepdad smoked. Daily. After dinner, after the kids were supposedly in bed, they'd get high together. The smell seeped under doors, through vents, into everything.

I knew that smell. It was the smell of my early childhood, of the caravan, of the reason I'd been taken away in the first place. And here it was again, in this house that looked so good on paper, in this family that had supposedly reformed.

The difference was discretion. Mum had learned, apparently, not to leave bongs lying around where social workers might see them. The habit hadn't changed; just the visibility. She'd gotten better at hiding it, at maintaining the facade.

I was seven. I didn't understand addiction yet, didn't have a framework for why someone would keep doing something that had already cost them so much. I just knew that the thing that had taken me away from Mum was still here, still present, still a secret kept from the people who'd decided to give me back.

It didn't take long for the cracks to show.

Mum was strict, yes. But strict in a way that felt reactive rather than consistent. Rules would appear from nowhere, punishments would be disproportionate, and the whole house walked on eggshells trying to figure out what would set her off on any given day.

And she was paranoid. About everything. About neighbours watching, about people talking, about threats that may or may not have been real. She'd get ideas in her head and they'd take root and grow until they crowded out everything else.

I didn't know words like "mental illness" or "anxiety disorder" or "trauma response." I just knew that my mother's brain worked differently than other people's brains. That she saw dangers that weren't there and missed dangers that were. That loving her was like loving the weather - you could never be sure what you were going to get.

Stepdad wasn't much better. He was quieter than Mum, less volatile on the surface, but there was something underneath. A tension. A coiled quality, like a spring held too tight. He and Mum argued constantly - behind closed doors, in hissed whispers, in the loaded silences that children learn to interpret better than words.

I'd lived in chaos before, but it was a different kind of chaos. Nan's house was neglect - absence, indifference, being left to fend for yourself. This house was something else. This was two adults locked in a battle that had nothing to do with the children caught in the crossfire.

Three months. That's how long it lasted.

The night we fled is a blur.

I don't remember what preceded it - what argument, what incident, what final straw. What I remember is Mum in a frenzy, packing bags, telling us to be quiet, to hurry, to not wake him. The fear in her voice, real or performed, I couldn't tell. The sense of urgency, of escape, of something terrible waiting if we didn't leave right now.

She said Stepdad was beating her. Had been beating her. That we weren't safe. That we had to go.

I was eight. I believed her. Why wouldn't I? She was my mother, and she was scared, and we were leaving in the middle of the night like refugees from our own home.

We flew back to Queensland. All of us - me, my sister, my baby brother. Landed on Nan's doorstep like we'd never left, like the whole Victoria experiment had been a dream that turned nightmare.

Nan took us in. Of course she did. More kids meant more payments, and besides, this was what family did. You opened your door when your daughter showed up fleeing her husband. You didn't ask too many questions. You just made room.

For about a week, we were refugees. Mum was the victim, Stepdad was the villain, and we were all safe now in Nan's housing commission house with its mismatched furniture and its smell of yesterday's cigarettes.

Then Stepdad arrived.

He'd followed us. Driven or flown or somehow made his way from Victoria to Queensland, and there he was, on Nan's doorstep, begging.

He'd change. He promised. He'd move to Queensland, away from his family, away from whatever had gone wrong down south. They'd start fresh. Try again. Make it work this time.

Mum listened. Mum forgave. Mum decided that yes, okay, they'd give it another shot.

I watched this happen with the confused understanding of a child who knows something is wrong but can't articulate what. We'd fled in the middle of the night. She'd said he was dangerous. And now she was taking him back, just like that, because he said he'd be different.

They made a plan. They'd fly back to Victoria together, close things up, sell the house or sort out whatever needed sorting. Then they'd return to Queensland and start over.

But there was a logistical problem. The kids. It would be easier, Mum said, if they didn't have to wrangle three children while dealing with everything in Victoria. Easier if someone stayed behind.

Someone. Not the little ones - they were hers, her do-over kids, the family she'd built with Stepdad. They'd go with her.

The someone who stayed behind was me.

"Watch her for a bit," Mum told Nan. "We'll be back soon. Just need to close things up."

They flew to Victoria. They left me behind.

I'd like to tell you I was surprised. That I felt betrayed, abandoned, shocked that my mother would leave me so casually after I'd only just arrived in her life.

But honestly? I don't remember feeling much of anything. This was how it worked. I'd learned that by eight. Adults made decisions, children went where they were told, and expecting anything different was a recipe for disappointment.

Nan, however, felt something. Nan felt opportunity.

Within a day of Mum leaving, Nan was on the phone to Child Services. Her daughter had abandoned a child with her. Just left her here, taken off to Victoria with the other kids, no plan, no timeline, no formal arrangement. This wasn't babysitting. This was abandonment.

The system cranked into action. Paperwork was filed. Custody was transferred. Nan was, once again, officially my carer. The payments resumed.

I don't know if Nan believed she was rescuing me or if she just saw an opportunity and grabbed it. Probably both. With Nan, motivations were always layered - genuine concern wrapped around self-interest wrapped around something darker.

Two weeks. That's all it took. Mum and Stepdad went to Victoria, sorted whatever they needed to sort, and came back. Two weeks.

But it was already too late. The paperwork was done. Custody had been transferred. Nan had moved fast, and the system had moved with her, and by the time Mum returned to Queensland expecting to collect her daughter, I wasn't hers to collect anymore.

Mum was furious. I remember the fighting. Mum and Nan, screaming at each other about custody and abandonment and who had the right to make decisions about me. Mum and Stepdad, continuing whatever war they'd been fighting in Victoria, just with a Queensland backdrop now. Everyone angry, everyone blaming everyone else, and me in the middle of it, trying to be invisible.

For a while, Mum and Stepdad lived in Nan's house. Downstairs, in some kind of makeshift arrangement that made everyone miserable. The house wasn't big enough for that many adults with that much conflict, but no one had anywhere else to go.

Eventually, they got their own place. Housing commission, of course. Back in the old neighbourhood, near Nan, near everything they'd supposedly escaped when they'd moved to Victoria. The fresh start had lasted three months. Now they were right back where they'd started, just with more kids and more damage.

I stayed with Nan.

It was decided, somehow, in the chaos of those weeks, that this was where I belonged. Mum had her hands full with the younger kids. Mum and Stepdad were still volatile, still figuring things out, still not stable enough to add another child to the mix. And besides, the custody paperwork was already done. Nan was my carer. The payments were flowing. Why disrupt what was working?

Working. That's what they called it. An eight-year-old shuttled between homes, belonging to neither, wanted by no one enough to fight for her.

Working.

The thing about being "looked awesome on paper" is that paper doesn't capture much.

It doesn't capture the pot smoke seeping under doors. It doesn't capture the paranoia, the arguments, the middle-of-the-night escapes. It doesn't capture a mother choosing her do-over family over her first mistake. It doesn't capture a grandmother weaponising bureaucracy to secure her income stream.

Paper captures checkboxes. House, husband, kids, job. Check, check, check, check.

I was a checkbox too. "Child returned to mother." Check. "Placement disrupted." Check. "Child returned to kinship care." Check.

My whole childhood, reduced to checkboxes. Moved around the board like a piece in a game I didn't understand, played by adults who couldn't see past the paperwork to the actual child underneath.

Awesome on paper.

Disaster in practice.

But the paper was what mattered. The paper was what got filed, what got funded, what got cited in meetings where my future was decided by people who'd never met me.

I was eight years old, and I'd already learned the most important lesson of my life: what things look like matters more than what things are.

It was a lesson I'd use later, when I built my own paper trail. My own checkboxes. My own version of "awesome on paper" that hid everything underneath.

But that was years away. For now, I was just a kid, back at Nan's, watching my mother drive away to her housing commission house with her real family, learning to be invisible again.

The system had tried. The system had failed. The system would try again.

It would keep failing.

But the paperwork would always look fine.

| 8 |

History Repeating

My Aunty was fourteen when history repeated itself.

I didn't understand it at the time. I was nine, and the adult dramas swirling around me were only partially visible. I caught glimpses, fragments, overheard conversations that I couldn't fully parse. But I knew something was happening with my Aunty. Something bad.

She'd started disappearing. Coming home late, or not coming home at all. Fighting with Nan constantly, screaming matches that shook the walls. There was a boyfriend, someone older, someone Nan didn't approve of. The details were kept from me, but the tension was impossible to miss.

We still shared a room, technically. But she was barely in it. She'd come home after I was asleep and leave before I woke up, or she wouldn't come home at all. Nan would rage and threaten and demand to know where she'd been. My Aunty would scream back, or say nothing at all, which was somehow worse.

I'd lie in my bed, in my corner of our shared room, and listen to them go at each other through the walls. The yelling was familiar - Nan was always yelling about something - but this was different. This had an edge to it. A desperation on both sides.

Then one night, we were in the car.

I don't remember why I was there, or where we'd been, or what had precipitated this particular crisis. What I remember is Nan driving, grim-faced and furious, heading toward the caravan park. The caravan park. The same one where my mother had been found at fourteen. The same one where I'd spent my earliest years. The same gravitational centre of family disaster that kept pulling us back.

There were police. Nan had called them, or they were already there, or they arrived at the same time we did - the sequence is blurry. What's clear is the scene: my Aunty being dragged out of a caravan by Nan and the cops, screaming, fighting, a fourteen-year-old girl who didn't want to be rescued.

I watched from the car. Nan had told me to stay put, and I did, face pressed to the window, watching my Aunty's life implode in real-time. She was crying. Nan was yelling. The police were doing that thing police do, authoritative and detached, handling a situation they'd probably handled a hundred times before.

A fourteen-year-old girl. A caravan. An older man.

Just like my mother, ten years earlier.

Just like always.

I thought about my mother that night. Nan dragging her out of a caravan when she was fourteen, pregnant with me, the man disappearing before dawn. And now here was Nan again, dragging another daughter out of another caravan, the same scene playing out like a song stuck on repeat.

What was it about this family and caravans? What was it about fourteen-year-old girls and older men and the same mistakes made over and over?

I was nine. I didn't have answers. I just had the image burned into my brain: my Aunty screaming, the police lights, Nan's face twisted with fury that might have been fear underneath. The knowledge that this had happened before and would probably happen again, because that's how cycles work. They cycle.

The man in the caravan was gone by the time we got there, or he made himself scarce when the police arrived. I never saw him. He was a ghost, like all the men in these stories - present long enough to do damage, then vanished before consequences could catch up.

My Aunty came home that night. She didn't have a choice. The police and Nan and the weight of her fourteen years made the decision for her. She was deposited back in the housing commission house, in the room we shared, in the life she'd been trying to escape.

She didn't speak to me. She didn't speak to anyone. She just lay on her bed, facing the wall, radiating fury and despair in equal measure.

I didn't know what to say. What do you say to someone who's just been dragged out of a caravan by her mother and the cops? I was a kid. I didn't have the framework to understand what I'd witnessed, only the visceral memory of it: the screaming, the police lights, the echo of my mother's story playing out again with a different daughter.

Things were different after that. My Aunty was watched more closely, her movements tracked, her freedom curtailed. Nan installed herself as warden, monitoring comings and goings, demanding to know where and when and with whom.

But you can't imprison a teenager in a housing commission house forever. The surveillance just made my Aunty more creative, more secretive, more determined to escape. Within a year, she'd leave home for good - at fifteen, barely older than my mother had been when she'd gotten pregnant with me. She found her own place, her own chaos, her own escape from Nan's control.

I don't know all the details of what happened to her after that. Our paths diverged. The family fractured along fault lines that had always been there, and everyone spun off into their own orbits. What I know is that she got out from under Nan's roof, and whatever came next, it was hers.

The cycle didn't break. It just kept spinning, catching each generation in turn.

And me? I stayed. Too young to run, too trapped to escape, too invisible to matter. I watched my Aunty leave and wondered when it would be my turn.

Years later, I got my file.

I've mentioned this before - the Freedom of Information request I submitted when I turned eighteen. The thick envelope of documents that laid out my childhood in bureaucratic detail. I requested it because I wanted to understand. I wanted to see what the system had seen, what they'd written down, what they'd known and done and failed to do.

What I found was worse than I expected.

The complaints were there. Documented. Exposed in clinical language that somehow made them more horrifying. My Aunty - the one I'd shared a room with, the one I'd watched get dragged out of the caravan - had been telling Child Services for years that Nan was beating her. Since she was twelve. Two years of reports, of allegations, of a child saying "help me" in the only official way she knew how.

She said Nan hit her. She said Nan had locked her in her room for two days and wouldn't let her out. She said things I hadn't known, hadn't seen, hadn't understood were happening in the same house where I was living.

Locked in her room for two days. I tried to picture it. Our room, the one we shared. Had I been there? Had I been sent somewhere else? I couldn't remember. But the report was clear: my Aunty had been imprisoned in her own bedroom, and someone had documented it.

And Child Services had done what they always did. They called Nan.

Imagine that. A child reports abuse, and the system's response is to call the abuser and give them a heads up. "Your daughter says you're beating her. Anything you'd like to say about that?"

My Aunty copped a beating for those reports. Of course she did. She'd tried to get help, and the help had made things worse, and she'd learned the lesson that all of us learned eventually: the system wasn't there to protect you. The system was there to manage paperwork.

It wasn't just my Aunty. My other Aunty - Aunty One, the oldest, the one who'd already left home by the time I arrived - she'd made complaints too. She told Child Services that I wasn't being fed properly. That I was eating pizza every night. That the house was a mess, that the conditions weren't suitable, that someone should do something.

Someone should do something. The eternal refrain of people who can see a problem but can't fix it themselves.

Child Services responded to these complaints with their standard protocol: a surprise visit. Except the surprise visits weren't surprises at all. They called ahead. They gave Nan warning. They scheduled their "unannounced" inspections with enough notice for her to prepare.

The notes in my file describe one of these visits. The social worker arrived and Nan met them on the stairs. Outside. She didn't let them in the house. She said she was enjoying the sun.

Enjoying the sun. Nan, who I never once saw voluntarily sit outside for leisure, was suddenly enjoying the sun on the exact day Child Services came to check on the living conditions.

The social worker wrote it down. "House likely messy." They noted that they hadn't been able to see inside. They documented their suspicion that something was being hidden. And then they... left. Drove away. Filed their report and moved on to the next case.

House likely messy. I lived in that house. I could have told them exactly how messy it was, and why, and what else was happening inside those walls. But no one asked me. I was just a child. My observations didn't count.

The file also contained notes about trying to get guardianship transferred to my mother. Discussions about whether Mum might be stable enough to take me back.

The conversations went nowhere. The current arrangement was "working." I was housed. I was enrolled in school. I was alive. The boxes were checked.

What the file revealed, more than anything, was the gap between what was known and what was done. The system had information. Multiple sources - my aunties, social workers, probably teachers and neighbours and anyone else paying attention - had flagged concerns. The documentation existed. The evidence was there.

And nothing changed.

I stayed with Nan. The payments kept flowing. The problems continued, invisible to everyone who had the power to stop it, visible only to the children who were living it.

Reading that file at eighteen was like watching a horror movie where you already know the ending. Every page, every report, every clinical notation was a moment where someone could have intervened and didn't. A trail of missed opportunities stretching back years.

The worst part wasn't what happened - I'd lived that, I knew what had happened. The worst part was seeing it written down, acknowledged, and ignored. The system had known. Not everything, but enough. They'd had the pieces. They just hadn't bothered to put them together.

Or maybe they had put them together and decided it wasn't worth the effort. Removing a child is hard. Paperwork, court dates, finding alternative placements. Leaving a child in a "kinship care" arrangement is easy. The family handles it. The payments are lower than foster care. The problem is contained.

I was a contained problem. Documented but not addressed. Known but not helped.

The only good thing - and I use "good" loosely here - was that Nan didn't hit me while they were around.

Small mercies. The system's bare minimum.

I think about my Aunty sometimes. The one I watched get dragged out of that caravan. She's still alive, still out there, still dealing with whatever that childhood made her. We don't talk. The family fractured long ago, everyone spinning off into their own orbits of dysfunction.

But I wonder if she ever got her file. If she ever read the reports she'd made as a twelve-year-old, begging for help that never came. If she knows how thoroughly she was failed.

I wonder if it would matter. Knowing doesn't change what happened. It just adds context to the damage. A frame around the wound.

And somewhere in the filing cabinets of Child Services, the paperwork accumulated, telling a story that everyone could read and no one would act on.

That's how it works when you're a kid in the system.

You're not a person. You're a file.

And files can be closed.

| 9 |

Up North

When I was twelve, we moved far north.

It happened suddenly, the way everything in my life happened. One day we were in the housing commission house with its familiar misery, and the next day Nan had a job offer and we were packing up and leaving. No discussion, no preparation, no asking how I felt about it. Just: we're going. Get your things.

The job was live-in housekeeper for a wealthy family. A proper family, with a proper house - not housing commission, not a rental, but a real home with land and space and money evident in every detail. They needed someone to cook and clean and manage the household, and somehow Nan had convinced them she was the right person for the job.

The irony wasn't lost on me, even at twelve. Nan, who never cooked for us, was going to cook for strangers. Nan, whose house was "likely messy" according to Child Services, was going to clean someone else's home. The woman who couldn't manage her own life was being paid to manage someone else's.

But that was Nan. She could perform competence when there was money involved. She could be whatever a situation required, as long as someone was paying for it. The version of herself she gave to employers was completely different from the version we got at home.

We moved into a small cottage on the property. It was included with the job - accommodation for the housekeeper and her dependents. After years of housing commission and caravans, it felt like a palace. Clean. Well-maintained. Surrounded by land instead of other people's dysfunction.

For a little while, it was almost good.

The family paid me to do small jobs. Taking out the rubbish, helping with yard work, little tasks that a twelve-year-old could handle. They didn't have to do this - I wasn't their employee, Nan was - but they were kind. They saw a kid who'd come with the housekeeper, and they found ways to include me.

The money was pocket change to them, probably. To me, it was revelation. I was earning. My own money, for my own work. The first time I'd ever had cash that was mine, that I'd gotten through effort rather than charity or government payments.

And they let me take horse riding lessons.

I need to pause here because this still feels surreal, even now. Horse riding lessons. Me. The kid from the housing commission, the kid who'd eaten charity furniture pizza for dinner, the kid whose file said "house likely messy" - I was learning to ride horses on a property where rich people lived.

The lessons weren't fancy. It was just the family's horses, and someone showing me the basics. But I loved it. The size of the animals, the power underneath you, the feeling of being in control of something bigger than yourself. For an hour at a time, I wasn't a kid in care, wasn't Nan's dependent, wasn't a file in a cabinet. I was just a girl on a horse, learning something new.

Those months up north were the closest thing to normal I'd experienced since the foster homes. Structure, stability, even a little bit of luxury. I started to relax. Started to think maybe this was it - maybe Nan had finally found something that worked, and we'd stay here, and things would be okay.

That was my mistake. Relaxing. Thinking things might be okay.

Nan had a boyfriend.

He appeared at some point during our time up north. I don't know where she met him or how long they'd been talking. He just showed up one day - a man, staying in our cottage, sleeping in Nan's room. Another adult in a rotating cast of adults who passed through our lives.

He stayed for about a week.

I don't know what happened between them. A fight, probably. Nan's relationships always ended in fights - screaming, accusations, doors slamming. Whatever it was, he left. Packed his things and disappeared, just like all the men in our family's stories.

And Nan lost her mind.

Not literally. Not in any way that would be documented or diagnosed. But something shifted after he left. The anger that was always simmering underneath broke through to the surface. She was volatile in a way I hadn't seen before - or maybe I had seen it, directed at my Aunty, but never at me.

I don't remember exactly what I did wrong. I think she asked me something and I didn't hear her. Or I heard her and didn't respond fast enough. Or I responded with the wrong tone, the wrong words, the wrong expression on my face. It could have been anything. When someone is looking for a reason to explode, any reason will do.

She grabbed my hair.

I remember that - the shock of her hand in my hair, gripping, pulling. I'd seen her hit my Aunty, but she'd never touched me like this. The payments, maybe. The knowledge that I was a Child Services case, that there was oversight, that bruises might be noticed. Whatever had protected me before wasn't protecting me now.

She dragged me by my hair to my bed, and she smashed my head into the side of it.

Not once. Over and over. The wooden frame of the bed against my skull, again and again, while she screamed things I can't remember because all I could hear was the impact and my own voice crying.

I don't know how long it lasted. Time does strange things when you're being hurt. It felt like forever. It probably wasn't. At some point she stopped, let go of my hair, walked away. Left me on the floor by my bed, sobbing, head throbbing, trying to understand what had just happened.

I had the next week off school.

That's how these things get hidden. You keep the kid home until the bruises fade, until the swelling goes down, until they can appear in public without questions being asked. Nan knew the protocol. She'd done this before - not to me, but to my Aunty. The same move, I'd later learn from the FOI file. Smashing heads into bed frames. Her signature.

I stayed in my room. I didn't tell anyone. Who would I tell? Child Services, who'd called Nan to warn her about surprise visits? The school, who'd accept whatever excuse she gave for my absence? There was no one. There had never been anyone.

I just waited for my face to heal and tried not to make her angry again.

Within six months, we were gone.

The departure was sudden, like everything else. One day we lived on this beautiful property with horses and pocket money and something resembling peace. The next day, Nan was packing in a frenzy, telling me to grab my things, we were leaving.

No notice to the employers. No explanation. Just a midnight flit - that's what they call it when you disappear owing money or obligations, when you run before consequences can catch you.

I didn't understand why at the time. The job had seemed fine. The family had been kind. Why were we running?

The story came out later, in pieces, the way family secrets always do. Someone tells someone who tells someone, and eventually the truth filters down to the kid who was never supposed to know.

Nan had told her employers she wanted to buy a house. She'd convinced them to be guarantors on a loan. They trusted her - she'd been working for them, living on their property, presenting the competent version of herself that she saved for paying customers. They signed the papers. Sixty thousand dollars.

She didn't buy a house.

She gambled it. All of it. Sixty thousand dollars, gone into poker machines or whatever her poison was. The money that was supposed to be a fresh start, a house, a future - fed into machines that gave nothing back.

And when the money was gone and the bills started coming, she ran.

Left her employers holding a sixty-thousand-dollar debt. Left the property trashed - I don't know the details, but I know the cottage wasn't in the state it had been when we arrived. Left everything behind and fled in the middle of the night, dragging me with her.

Back to Brisbane. Back to a caravan park. Back to exactly where we'd started, minus the money and the job and any pretense that things might get better.

Sixty thousand dollars. In the early nineties, you could buy a house for that. A real house, owned outright, no mortgage. Nan had held that possibility in her hands and shoved it into a machine that played cheerful sounds while it ate her future.

Our future. My future.

Not that I had any say in it. I was cargo. I went where I was taken.

The caravan park felt like defeat.

After the property up north, after the horses and the cottage and the brief glimpse of a different life, returning to a caravan was crushing. The smallness. The communal bathrooms. The neighbours close enough to hear through thin walls. Everything I thought I'd escaped, welcoming me back like an old friend who wasn't actually a friend at all.

Nan acted like nothing had happened. That was her way - chaos, disaster, upheaval, and then a reset, as if the slate had been wiped clean. No discussion of the job we'd fled, the money she'd stolen, the people she'd defrauded. Just forward motion, always forward motion, outrunning the past without ever acknowledging it.

But I remembered. The head against the bed frame. The week off school. The midnight departure and the sixty thousand dollars that had evaporated into nothing.

I was twelve years old, and I finally understood what my grandmother really was.

Not just neglectful. Not just loud and scary. She was dangerous. She was a fraud. She was someone who would hurt you and steal from kind people and run from consequences, and she would do it again because it was who she was.

And I was stuck with her. For three more years, at least, until I was old enough to leave. Three more years of caravans and chaos and walking on eggshells, trying not to trigger another explosion.

Three more years of surviving Nan.

After we came back, I did something I'd never done before. I went to Child Services myself.

I don't remember exactly how I got there - whether I walked, took a bus, asked someone for help. But I remember sitting in an office, talking to an adult with a notepad, telling them what had happened up north. The head into the bed frame. The violence. The fear.

I asked to be rehomed. Those were my exact words, I think. Rehomed. Like I was a dog who'd ended up with the wrong owner.

"I want to go anywhere," I told them. "Anywhere but with her."

They wrote it down. They nodded sympathetically. They said they'd look into it.

They didn't rehome me.

I don't know why. Budget constraints, lack of placements, the preference for kinship care that kept kids with family even when family was the problem. Maybe they called Nan and she talked her way out of it. Maybe they decided a twelve-year-old's word wasn't enough. Maybe my file was too thick and I was too complicated and it was easier to close the conversation than open an investigation.

Whatever the reason, I walked out of that office and went back to Nan. Back to the caravan. Back to the life I'd just officially asked to escape.

The system had failed me again. But by now, I was used to it.

Failure was the only thing the system reliably delivered.

Two more years in that caravan park. Two more years of Nan and her moods and her parade of bad decisions. Two more years of being invisible, staying quiet, not giving her a reason.

She didn't hit me again - not like that, not the head into the bed frame. Maybe she'd scared herself. Maybe she was being more careful now that I'd reported it. Or maybe she just didn't have a boyfriend leave her again, didn't have that particular trigger pulled.

But I never forgot. I never trusted her again. Whatever relationship we'd had - if you can call it a relationship, this thing between a child and the adult who received money to house her - it was different now. She was someone to be managed, avoided, endured. Not family. Not safe. Just a situation I had to survive until I could get out.

The countdown had started.

I just had to make it a few more years.

| 10 |

The Good Aunty

When I was fourteen, Child Services finally did their job.

I don't know what changed. Maybe my report from two years earlier had stayed in the file, accumulating weight alongside all the other complaints. Maybe a new social worker looked at my case with fresh eyes and saw what others had missed. Maybe the system just randomly decided to function for once.

Whatever the reason, the decision came down: I was being removed from Nan's care.

The relief was physical. I remember my whole body unclenching when they told me, muscles I didn't know I'd been holding tight for years suddenly releasing. It was over. The caravans, the chaos, the walking on eggshells, the fear of triggering another explosion. Over.

But relief came with a question: where would I go?

Not back to Mum - she was still in her housing commission house with Stepdad and my siblings, still in the same volatile situation that had made her unsuitable years ago. Not to foster care - I was fourteen now, too old for the easy placements, too much history in my file. The system preferred family when family was available.

And family was available. Aunty One - Nan's oldest daughter, the one who'd escaped years ago, the one who'd made complaints about my care - she was willing to take me.

Willing. That word again. But this time it felt different. This time it felt like it might actually mean something.

Aunty One had done everything right.

She'd gotten out of Nan's house young and never looked back. She'd met someone decent, married him, had kids of her own. They'd bought a house - actually bought it, with a mortgage and payments and their names on a deed. She had a job. He had a job. They were stable in a way that no one else in our family had ever managed.

She was proof that the cycle could be broken. That growing up with Nan didn't have to define your whole life. That you could choose differently, build differently, become someone other than what your childhood had made you.

I'd met her before, of course. Family gatherings, occasional visits, the scattered contact that happened when relatives lived in the same city but different worlds. She'd always been kind to me - a warm presence in a sea of chaos, someone who looked at me like I was a person rather than a problem.

And now I was going to live with her.

The house was in a nice suburb. Not rich, but respectable. Lawns were mowed. Cars worked. Neighbours waved at each other and meant it. The contrast with the housing commission streets I'd grown up on was stark - this was what normal looked like, what working hard and making good choices could build.

I had my own room.

I need to sit with this for a moment, because even now it feels significant. My own room. Not shared with an Aunty who resented me, not a corner of a caravan, not a temporary arrangement in someone else's space. A room that was mine.

And she decorated it.

Before I arrived, Aunty One had prepared the room for me. Painted it, I think, or at least made it fresh. There was a bed with proper bedding - not charity donations, but things she'd chosen, that matched, that were meant for me. There were curtains on the windows. A desk for homework. Space for my things, what little I had.

A room that said: you live here now. You belong here. You matter.

I stood in the doorway and didn't know what to do. How do you respond to kindness when you've mostly known its absence? How do you trust a good thing when good things have always been temporary?

I cried, I think. Or maybe I didn't. Maybe I just stood there, frozen, trying to recalibrate my entire understanding of how life could work.

Living with Aunty One was like visiting a foreign country where everything was better but nothing made sense.

There were routines. Dinner happened at dinner time, at a table, with food she'd cooked. Breakfast happened in the morning. People said good morning and good night and asked how your day was and actually listened to the answer.

There were rules, but they were consistent. Not the arbitrary explosions of Nan's house, where punishment depended on mood rather than behaviour. At Aunty One's, you knew what was expected. You knew what would happen if you didn't meet expectations. The system was predictable, which made it navigable.

Her kids - my cousins - were younger than me. They'd grown up in this house, with these routines, never knowing anything different. They took it for granted, the way you take gravity for granted. Of course dinner happens at a table. Of course Mum cooks. Of course everything is clean and calm and safe.

I watched them like an anthropologist studying a foreign tribe. So this is how the other half lives. This is what happens when the cycle breaks. This is what I could have had, if things had been different.

The envy was complicated. I didn't begrudge them their good life - they were kids, innocent, not responsible for the accident of their birth. But I felt the gap acutely. Every normal moment in that house reminded me of all the normal moments I'd missed.

Aunty One had nice things.

This is where my story gets uncomfortable. Where I have to admit to behaviour I'm not proud of, choices that still make me cringe when I think about them.

She had nice clothes. Nice jewellery. Things she'd worked for, saved for, accumulated over years of being a responsible adult. Things that represented everything I'd never had and desperately wanted.

And I wanted to be liked at school.

This is hard to explain if you've never been the kid from nowhere, the kid with nothing, the kid who shows up in hand-me-downs while everyone else has the right brands, the right accessories, the right everything. The social currency of high school is stuff. What you wear, what you have, what you can show off. And I had nothing.

So I borrowed things.

That's what I told myself. Borrowed. Not stole - borrowed. I'd take something of Aunty One's, wear it to school, feel normal for a day, feel like I belonged. The plan was always to return it, to slip it back where I'd found it before anyone noticed.

But I was careless. Or maybe I wanted to get caught. Maybe some part of me was testing this new situation, pushing to see when the other shoe would drop, when the kindness would reveal itself as temporary.

I wore a piece of her jewellery to school and forgot to take it off before I got home. She saw it. She knew it was hers.

The confrontation I expected never came. There was no screaming, no violence, no bags packed on the doorstep. Aunty One just... noticed. And knew.

I spent the next couple of weeks terrified.

I stayed in my room as much as possible, avoiding her, avoiding everyone. Waiting for the punishment that had to be coming. In Nan's house, something like this would have triggered a nuclear response - yelling, hitting, weeks of cold fury. I braced myself for the explosion.

It never came.

Instead, there was Christmas.

I don't remember if my theft was directly addressed. Maybe there was a conversation I've blocked out, or maybe Aunty One decided to handle it differently. What I remember is Christmas morning, sitting with the family, opening presents.

She gave me a ring.

A ring of my own. Not borrowed, not stolen - given. A piece of jewellery that was mine, that I didn't have to take because someone had chosen to give it to me.

I felt like the worst person in the world.

Here was this woman who'd taken me in, decorated a room for me, fed me, included me in her family. And I'd repaid her by stealing. By being exactly the kind of person everyone probably expected me to be - the kid from the bad family, the kid from the system, the kid who couldn't be trusted.

She'd responded to my betrayal with generosity. With a gift that said: I know what you did, and I'm choosing kindness anyway. I'm choosing to give you what you were trying to take.

I should have been grateful. I should have seen this as the turning point, the moment where I decided to be better, to deserve the chance I'd been given.

Instead, I ran.

Christmas Day, I was supposed to go to Mum's for a visit. A sleep-over with my siblings, the kind of normal family interaction that the system encouraged. Stay connected. Maintain bonds. Pretend we were all one big functional unit.

I went. But I didn't come back.

Lying in Mum's housing commission house that night, surrounded by my siblings, I made a decision. I wasn't going back to Aunty One's. I couldn't face her. Couldn't face the kindness I didn't deserve, the decorated room that felt like a reproach, the evidence of my own failure.

It made no sense. I was running from the best situation I'd ever been in, toward a house I knew was dysfunctional. I was choosing chaos over stability, damage over healing, the familiar over the good.

But that's what trauma does. It rewires your brain until safety feels dangerous and danger feels like home. I didn't have the words for it then. I just knew I couldn't stay somewhere that made me feel so exposed, so seen, so unworthy.

I told Mum I wanted to live with her. I told Child Services I wanted to live with her. I said I just wanted to be a normal kid, with my normal family, in a normal house.

Aunty One told them I was running away. She was right. I was absolutely running away. From her kindness, from my shame, from the possibility that I might actually be okay.

Child Services, faced with a fourteen-year-old who wanted to live with her mother and a mother who was willing to take her, did what they always did. They took the path of least resistance. Paperwork was filed. Placement was changed. I was Mum's problem now.

I wish I could go back in time and slap that stupid girl. Shake her. Make her see what she was throwing away and what she was running toward.

But you can't go back. You can only go forward, carrying the weight of your choices.

I chose Mum and Stepdad.

I chose wrong.

Aunty One let me go.

She didn't fight it, didn't try to force me to stay. Maybe she understood something I didn't - that you can't make someone accept help, can't force someone to heal. Maybe she was just tired. Taking in a traumatised teenager is hard enough when they want to be there. Taking in one who's actively fleeing your kindness is impossible.

I saw her a few times after that, over the years. The relationship never recovered. She'd offered me everything, and I'd thrown it back in her face. That kind of rejection leaves marks on both sides.

She's one of the family members I don't talk to anymore. Not because she did anything wrong - she did everything right. But being around her reminds me of who I was at fourteen, the choices I made, the chance I squandered.

Some bridges don't just burn. They collapse under the weight of your own stupidity, and you stand on the other side watching the wreckage, knowing you're the one who brought it down.

I learned something important from that experience, though I didn't understand it until much later.

I learned that I was capable of sabotaging my own happiness. That when good things came, some part of me would find a way to destroy them. That I'd been so shaped by chaos that stability felt like a threat to be neutralised.

This pattern would repeat throughout my life. Good job? Find a way to lose it. Good relationship? Find a way to ruin it. Good situation? Run from it toward something worse.

The therapists would probably call it self-sabotage, or repetition compulsion, or some other clinical term. I just call it the training I received. When your childhood teaches you that good things don't last, you learn to end them yourself. At least that way you're in control.

Aunty One's house was the first time I consciously chose destruction over possibility. It wouldn't be the last.

But standing in Mum's housing commission kitchen, newly arrived, freshly escaped from kindness, I didn't know any of that yet.

I just knew I was home.

And I was about to learn exactly what that meant.

| 11 |

Back to Mum

Mum had rules.

This was the first thing I noticed, moving into her housing commission house at fourteen. Rules everywhere, for everything, enforced with a rigidity that felt almost military. Bedtimes. Chores. Ways of speaking, ways of behaving, ways of existing in her space that I had to learn quickly or face consequences.

After Nan's chaos, you'd think I'd appreciate structure. And maybe I would have, if the structure had made sense. But Mum's rules weren't about creating stability - they were about control. She needed to know where everyone was, what everyone was doing, that her authority was absolute and unquestioned.

I was a teenager. Questioning authority was basically my job description.

The punishment for rule-breaking was the cane.

I don't mean a metaphorical cane, some abstract threat held over my head. I mean an actual cane - thin, flexible, the kind that whistles through the air before it connects. When I did something wrong, the ritual was always the same: hand on the table, palm up, and the cane wrapped across my knuckles.

It hurt. It was meant to hurt. That was the point.

Looking back, I can see that Mum was trying to be a parent in the only way she knew how. She'd grown up with Nan, which meant she'd grown up with violence as discipline. She was replicating what she'd learned, probably thinking she was being reasonable, controlled, measured. At least she wasn't smashing heads into bed frames.

But the cane was still violence. The fear was still fear. And living in that house meant living with a constant low-grade anxiety, always calculating which rules I might be breaking, always bracing for the whistle and the sting.

Stepdad was worse.

Not in the obvious ways - he didn't hit me, didn't do the cane ritual. His violence was different. Explosive. Unpredictable. The kind that came out of nowhere and destroyed everything in its path.

He and Mum fought constantly. The arguments would start small - a comment, a look, something insignificant that caught fire and spread. Within minutes they'd be screaming at each other, saying things that couldn't be unsaid, filling the house with a tension so thick you could choke on it.

And then it would turn physical.

I didn't see all of it. Some of it happened behind closed doors, in their bedroom, muffled but audible. But I saw enough. I saw the aftermath, at least. The holes in the hallway walls.

Most people, seeing holes in walls, would assume someone had been punching them. Angry man, clenched fist, drywall giving way. That's the normal assumption.

These holes weren't from fists.

They were from my mother's head.

Stepdad would grab her and slam her into the wall hard enough to break through. Again and again, down the hallway, a trail of damage that mapped his rage. The walls of that housing commission house were a record of violence, a connect-the-dots of my mother's skull against plaster.

I was fourteen, fifteen. Old enough to understand what I was seeing, too young to do anything about it. I'd hear it start - the yelling, the escalation, the sounds that meant it had gone physical - and I'd freeze. Fight, flight, or freeze, and I always froze.

Except once.

One night it was bad. Worse than usual. The sounds coming from down the hall were different - more desperate, more sustained. My sister was crying, really crying, the kind of crying that meant she was scared beyond comfort.

I grabbed her.

I don't know where the courage came from. I just knew I had to get her out of there, had to take her somewhere safe, somewhere away from the sounds of our mother being hurt.

I took her next door. To the neighbours. Knocked on their door with my little sister sobbing against my hip and tried to explain that we needed help, that something was wrong at our house, that we needed somewhere to be.

They let us in. For a few minutes, we were safe.

Then Stepdad came.

He'd finished with Mum, apparently. Noticed we were gone. Came to collect us. He pounded on the neighbours' door, demanded we come out, and when they opened it, he grabbed us and dragged us home.

Dragged. My sister screaming, me stumbling, trying to keep up with his grip on my arm. Back across the yard, back into the house, back into the situation I'd tried to escape.

Nobody did anything.

The neighbours didn't call the police. They didn't intervene. They just watched us get dragged away and closed their door.

I used to be angry about that. How could they just stand there? How could they let two kids get hauled back into a house where violence was obviously happening?

But I understand it now. This was a housing commission street. Every house had its own disaster. Violence wasn't unusual - it was Tuesday. Getting involved meant making enemies, meant drama, meant potentially becoming a target yourself. People kept their heads down and their doors closed because that's how you survived in places like that.

The system had built a neighbourhood where abuse was normalised, then acted surprised when no one reported it.

I was a typical teenager, which meant I was a mess.

My room was perpetually disastrous. Clothes on the floor, stuff everywhere, the chaos that happens when you're fifteen and have never been taught how to maintain a space and don't particularly care to learn. It drove Mum crazy, which was probably part of the point.

One day I came home from hanging out with friends. Walking up to the house, I could see something was wrong. There was stuff on the side of the house. Piled up against the wall, spilling onto the grass.

My stuff.

Everything I owned. Every possession I'd accumulated over fifteen years of life - which wasn't much, but it was mine. Clothes, books, random treasures, the small collection of things that made up my material existence. All of it was outside, thrown there, discarded like garbage.

Stepdad had decided to teach me a lesson about keeping my room clean. His method was to open my window and throw everything I owned through it.

I stood there looking at the pile. Some things were broken - items that couldn't survive being hurled from a window onto concrete. Precious things, irreplaceable things, the few objects I actually cared about. Destroyed.

I didn't cry. I didn't scream. I just started picking things up and carrying them back inside. Put them away in my room, cleaned up the mess, tried to repair what could be repaired.

What else could I do? Make a scene? Confront him? I'd seen what happened to people who confronted Stepdad. The walls told that story clearly enough.

I just absorbed it. Added it to the list. Kept my head down and my mouth shut and waited for the next thing.

The next thing came soon enough.

The toilet.

I still can't quite believe this is how it ended. After everything - the cane, the violence, the belongings thrown through windows - the thing that finally got me kicked out was needing to use the bathroom.

It was a weekend. Stepdad was in the toilet. I needed to go. Badly. The kind of urgent need that makes you shift from foot to foot, doing the uncomfortable dance of a full bladder.

I waited outside the door. Did the dance. Made it obvious, probably, that I was in distress.

And Stepdad, inside the bathroom, decided that my waiting was a personal attack.

He came out furious. Accused me of doing it deliberately, of trying to make his life difficult, of being disrespectful, of whatever imaginary crime my bladder had committed against him. The argument escalated, as arguments in that house always did.

By the end of it, I was out.

Not just sent to my room. Not just punished. Out. Kicked out of the house. At fifteen years old, for the crime of needing to pee while my stepfather was in the bathroom.

I went to a friend's house. Her parents took me in, let me stay, treated me with more kindness than my own family had shown. They wanted to keep me - actually wanted me, actually offered to let me live with them, to become part of their family.

But Child Services had other ideas. A meeting was required. Reconciliation had to be attempted. My mother and stepfather had to be given the opportunity to explain themselves.

The meeting was in a Child Services office. Me on one side, Mum and Stepdad on the other, a social worker in the middle trying to mediate a situation that was beyond mediation.

They took turns describing everything that was wrong with me.

I was difficult. I was disrespectful. I was messy, ungrateful, impossible to live with. I caused problems. I created tension. I was the source of every difficulty in their household, and they'd tried so hard, and I'd made it impossible.

Stepdad claimed that random people drove past him on the street and told him to "lay off" me. I don't know if this was true or a paranoid invention. In his telling, he was the victim - persecuted for trying to discipline a wayward child, harassed by strangers who didn't understand what he was dealing with.

And then Mum spoke.

She said it was her time now. Those words exactly, burned into my memory and confirmed later in my FOI file. Her time. She was going back to school - as a mature-age student, at my high school - and she needed to focus on herself. On her future. On building something that was hers.

I was a distraction. A reminder. Every day at school, she'd have to see me, and seeing me would remind her of things she wanted to forget. The teenage pregnancy, the failed early motherhood, all the reasons I'd been taken away in the first place. I was evidence of her worst years, walking around the same hallways, making it impossible for her to reinvent herself.

She demanded that they move me to a different school. Get me out of her sight. Let her have her fresh start without my face constantly reminding her that she'd been a disaster long before she was a student.

The social worker wrote all this down. I know because I read it later, in my file. The clinical documentation of my mother choosing herself over me, in a government office, with witnesses.

I sat there and cried.

When they asked me what I wanted, I couldn't speak. I just said, through tears, that I didn't want to leave my school. I didn't want to leave my friends. They were all I had. The only stable thing in my life, the only people who cared about me, and now my mother wanted to take them away too.

It didn't matter. My tears didn't matter. My preferences didn't matter. The decision had already been made.

I was going back to Nan.

Back to the caravan park. Back to the woman who'd smashed my head into a bed frame. Back to the situation I'd escaped two years earlier, when Child Services had finally done their job and removed me.

Full circle. Complete rotation of the carousel.

Mum got her wish. She went back to school, walked those hallways without having to see me, reinvented herself into whatever she wanted to be. I don't know if she graduated. I don't know if the fresh start worked. By that point, I'd stopped caring.

Stepdad got his wish too. The difficult child was gone, the household was simpler, the target of his rage had been removed. I'm sure he found other targets - the walls, my siblings, my mother. Violence doesn't go away when you remove one victim. It just redirects.

And I got the caravan park. Nan's familiar chaos. The place I'd spent so much of my childhood, the place I'd begged Child Services to save me from, the place they kept sending me back to like a package that couldn't find its destination.

The system had managed, in the space of two years, to take me from the best situation I'd ever been in and deposit me in the worst. Aunty One's decorated room to Nan's caravan. Kindness to cruelty. Possibility to poverty.

And all I'd had to do was need to use the toilet.

After Stepdad died, years later, Mum apologised.

She said she was sorry for all of it. The kicking out, the meeting, the demand that I be erased from her school. She said it wasn't her - it was him. Stepdad had wanted me gone, and she'd just found ways to make it happen. She was the victim too, controlled by a violent man, doing what she had to do to survive.

I listened to her apology. I heard her explanation. I understood, intellectually, that she'd been in a terrible situation herself, that abuse warps your judgment, that survival sometimes means sacrificing others.

I didn't forgive her.

I still haven't.

Because here's the thing: she packed those bags. She found those excuses. She sat in that meeting and said "it's my time now" and demanded I be removed from her school so she wouldn't have to look at me. No one held a gun to her head and made her say those words.

She chose herself. Every time, in every situation, when it came down to me or her, she chose herself.

And I was fifteen years old, crying in a Child Services office, asking only to keep my friends.

Some things you don't forgive. Some things you just carry, and try not to let them define you, and build a life anyway.

But you don't forgive.

Not really.

Not ever.

| 12 |

Freefall

Back at Nan's. Back in the caravan park. Fifteen years old with nothing but a garbage bag of clothes and a clear understanding that nobody wanted me.

I finished grade ten. That was the goal I set for myself - just get through, just complete this one thing, just have something to show for fifteen years of chaos. I wasn't doing well academically. Hard to focus on homework when your home situation is a caravan with a grandmother who might explode at any moment. But I showed up. I sat in classes. I did the minimum.

When grade ten ended, I made a decision: I was done with school.

The logic seemed sound at the time. I wasn't learning anything useful. I wasn't going to university - that was for people with stable homes and supportive families and futures that extended beyond next week. What I needed was money. Money changed everything. Money was the difference between Sarah's house and Nan's caravan. Money was freedom.

So I got a job.

My first real job was at a discount store. The kind of place that sold everything cheap - homewares, clothes, random plastic things nobody needed but everyone bought. Minimum wage, irregular hours, fluorescent lighting that made everyone look slightly ill.

I was terrible at it.

Not at the work itself, which wasn't complicated. Stack shelves, work the register, smile at customers, repeat. I could do those things. What I couldn't do was show up consistently, on time, ready to work.

I'd stay out late and be too tired to wake up. I'd call in sick when I wasn't sick, just because I didn't feel like going. I'd find excuses, always excuses, reasons why today wasn't a good day, why I needed just one more day off, why surely they'd understand.

They didn't understand. They fired me.

I told myself it wasn't my fault. The job was boring. The pay was crap. The managers were unfair. I had a whole narrative about why the problem was them, not me.

The next job ended the same way. And the one after that.

Three months. That was my pattern. I'd get hired, work for about three months, and then either get fired or quit. Sometimes they'd just stop giving me shifts until I got the message. Sometimes I'd decide the job was too hard, too boring, too whatever, and walk away.

I had no work ethic. That's the brutal truth. I'd never learned how to show up, day after day, and do something you didn't feel like doing. Nan hadn't modeled it - she worked when she felt like it and scammed when she didn't. Mum hadn't modeled it either. Nobody had ever taught me that work was something you did regardless of mood, that reliability mattered, that your feelings about a job were irrelevant to whether you did it.

I just thought I could want my way to success. Work hard, Sarah's mum had said. I thought that meant working when I felt motivated. It actually meant working when I didn't.

That lesson would take years to learn.

Money came in and money went out, faster than it came.

I was a spender. A shopper. The moment cash hit my hand, it was already spent - on clothes, on things for friends, on anything shiny that caught my eye. The concept of saving, of putting money aside for later, of delayed gratification - these were foreign ideas. I'd grown up in scarcity, and scarcity teaches you to grab what you can while you can, because it won't be there tomorrow.

I bought things for friends. That was a big one. I wanted to be liked, wanted to be generous, wanted to be the person who showed up with gifts. If buying people things made them happy, I'd buy things until my wallet was empty. And then I'd wonder why I couldn't afford rent.

Budgeting wasn't a skill I possessed. Nobody had taught me. You can't learn financial literacy from people who've never had finances to be literate about. I just spent until the money was gone, then scrambled until more money arrived, then spent that too.

The cycle of poverty isn't just about not having money. It's about not having the skills to manage money when you get it. I was living proof.

Boys were another disaster.

I started dating around this time - if you can call it dating. It was more like a series of collisions with males who wanted one thing and weren't interested in offering anything else.

I didn't know what a healthy relationship looked like. I'd seen Mum and Stepdad, which was violence and control. I'd seen Nan's revolving door of men who stayed briefly and left messily. I'd seen my aunties make the same mistakes over and over - caravans and older men and cycles that never broke.

What I hadn't seen was partnership. Respect. Two people who actually liked each other and treated each other well. That was theoretical, something from movies, not something that happened in real life.

So I accepted whatever I got. Boys who just wanted sex. Boys who disappeared after getting it. Boys who treated me like I was disposable, because I acted like I was disposable, because that's what I believed about myself.

Contraception wasn't something anyone talked about. Not Nan, not Mum, not the boys who certainly weren't going to bring it up. I knew, in a vague way, that sex could lead to pregnancy. I knew I didn't want kids - I was terrified of becoming my mother, of screwing up a child the way I'd been screwed up. But knowing and doing are different things, and in the chaos of those years, I wasn't exactly making careful choices.

I was self-aware enough to see the problems. That was the strange thing. I could watch myself making bad decisions, could narrate the disaster as it unfolded, could see exactly where I was going wrong. But seeing it didn't translate to stopping it. The pattern was too strong, the pull too heavy. I was a passenger in my own life, watching the crash happen in slow motion.

One of the boyfriends smoked pot.

This shouldn't have been notable - everyone I knew smoked pot, it seemed like. Nan smoked. Mum smoked. Half the caravan park was perpetually hazy with it. Marijuana was as normal as cigarettes in my world, just something adults did to take the edge off.

But I'd never tried it myself. Some combination of not wanting to be like them and not having the opportunity and maybe just luck. I'd made it to sixteen without smoking anything.

The boyfriend thought this was weird. Uncool. He wanted me to try it, to be part of his world, to share the experience with him. And I wanted to be cool, wanted to fit in, wanted him to like me.

So I tried it.

It made me sick. Really sick. Not the pleasant haze everyone talked about, not the mellow relaxation, just nausea and dizziness and the immediate knowledge that this was not for me. My body rejected it completely, like it was allergic to the thing that had derailed my mother's life.

I never smoked again. That's one bad choice I managed to avoid, purely through biological rejection rather than wisdom.

By sixteen, I was done with Queensland.

Nan was Nan. The caravan park was the caravan park. The jobs came and went and never led anywhere. The boyfriends used me and left. Everything felt stuck, circular, like I was running on a wheel that went nowhere.

Mum and Stepdad were back in Victoria by then. Country town, far from everything, starting over again. They'd moved back after the housing commission years, trying for another fresh start. From a distance, it looked like escape. Like maybe things could be different somewhere else.

So I decided to follow them.

I booked a bus ticket. Greyhound, all the way from Brisbane to country Victoria. Eighteen hours on a bus, watching the landscape change, heading toward something that couldn't possibly be worse than what I was leaving.

I didn't tell Nan. Just made my plans quietly, packed my things, prepared to disappear.

But the bus company called to confirm the booking. Standard procedure. And Nan answered the phone.

She didn't try to stop me. That wasn't her style. Instead, she booked a ticket for herself. Same bus. Same destination.

I thought I was escaping her. Turned out she was coming with me.

Arriving in Victoria with Nan in tow was not what I'd planned.

Mum and Stepdad were furious. They'd agreed to let me stay - reluctantly, probably, but they'd agreed. They had not agreed to Nan suddenly appearing on their doorstep, suitcase in hand, expecting accommodation.

But what could they do? She was there. She needed somewhere to stay. Family was family, even when family was a nightmare.

Nan found a granny flat to rent pretty quickly. She was good at that - landing on her feet, finding situations, surviving through sheer force of will. Within a week she was set up in her own place, close enough to be a presence but not actually living with Mum.

I stayed with Mum and Stepdad. Got a local job, something minimum wage and forgettable. Tried to settle into this new life in this new place, far from everything I'd known.

It lasted about as long as everything else. A few months of pretending things were normal. A few months of walking on eggshells in a house where violence still simmered beneath the surface, just quieter now, just more controlled.

And then my past caught up with me.

Back in Queensland, I'd gotten pregnant.

The boyfriend - not the pot smoker, a different one - and I had been careless. Of course we'd been careless. Sixteen years old, no education about contraception, no real understanding of consequences. The pregnancy wasn't planned, wasn't wanted, wasn't anything but terrifying.

I'd miscarried. Alone, scared, not really understanding what was happening to my body. It was traumatic in ways I didn't process until years later. At the time, I just felt relief mixed with grief mixed with confusion. A pregnancy that ended before it began. A bullet dodged, maybe. Or a loss. I still don't know how to categorize it.

I'd told the boyfriend. Mistake. I'd thought he should know, thought we were in something together, thought honesty was the right choice.

He ran. Disappeared from my life the moment he heard the word "pregnant," even though the pregnancy was already over. But before he ran, he did one last thing.

He found out where I'd gone. Tracked down my mother's address in Victoria. And he told them.

I came home from work one day to find my bags packed and sitting on the doorstep.

Again. The same scene, different house, different state. My belongings in garbage bags, waiting by the door, the universal signal that I was no longer welcome.

Mum had found out about the pregnancy. The miscarriage. The boyfriend. All of it, delivered by someone who wanted to hurt me, and succeeding.

She didn't ask if I was okay. Didn't ask what had happened, how I was feeling, whether I needed help processing what I'd been through. She just saw the information as evidence of who I was - damaged, shameful, too much trouble to keep around.

I was sent away. An hour from Mum's house, to a halfway house for young people who had nowhere else to go.

Sixteen years old. Alone in a strange town. Living in institutional housing because my family had run out of places to put me.

I think about that sometimes. The pattern.

Mum's response to every problem was the same: remove me. First the toilet incident, bags on the doorstep, kicked out at fifteen. Now this - a traumatic experience I'd already survived alone, weaponized against me, resulting in exile.

She never asked questions. Never tried to understand. Never sat down and said "what happened?" or "are you okay?" or "how can I help?" Her only parenting tool was removal. When I became inconvenient, I got erased.

After Stepdad died, she apologized for this too. Said he made her do it. Said she was just trying to survive, trying to keep the peace, trying to manage an impossible situation.

And maybe that's true. Maybe she was a victim too, controlled by a violent man, doing what she had to do.

But she picked up that phone when the ex-boyfriend called. She listened to his story. She packed those bags and put them on the doorstep. She sent her sixteen-year-old daughter to a halfway house an hour away, alone, after a miscarriage.

No one made her do that. That was a choice. Her choice.

She's not forgiven for that either.

The halfway house was exactly what it sounds like. A place between places. A holding pen for young people who'd fallen through every crack in every system.

There were rules, structure, people who checked on you. Social workers and support staff and programs designed to help you get back on your feet. It wasn't terrible. It was just... temporary. Transitional. A pause before whatever came next.

I was sixteen years old. I'd been abused by my grandmother, kicked out by my mother twice, failed by a system that was supposed to protect me, betrayed by a boyfriend who should have kept his mouth shut.

I had no education beyond grade ten. No job skills that mattered. No money saved. No family I could count on. No plan for what came next.

I was at the bottom. The absolute bottom, as far as I could tell.

But here's the thing about bottoms: they're also foundations. They're the place where you stop falling and start building. They're where you finally run out of people to blame and start looking at yourself.

I didn't know that yet. I was sixteen, alone, scared, and angry at everyone who'd put me there.

But somewhere in that halfway house, something shifted. Some tiny part of me started to wonder if maybe - just maybe - I could build something different.

It would take years. It would take more failures, more bad choices, more rock bottoms that turned out not to be the actual bottom after all.

But the thought was there, planted like a seed in bad soil.

Maybe I could be someone else.

Maybe I could get out.

| 13 |

The Chaos Twin

The halfway house wasn't a destination. It was a waiting room.

After a few months of institutional living, I decided to go back to Queensland. Victoria had nothing for me - just Mum who didn't want me, Nan who'd followed me like a curse, and a country town full of strangers. At least in Queensland I knew the landscape. Knew which disasters were which.

I called Aunty Two. The one I'd shared a room with at Nan's, the one I'd watched get dragged from a caravan at fourteen, the one who'd escaped Nan's house at fifteen and built her own chaotic life. She was an adult now, with kids of her own, a single mum making it work however she could.

She said I could come stay with her. Help with the kids. She worked nights; I could work days. We'd make it work.

So I went. Another bus ride, another relocation, another attempt at something that might be stability.

Aunty Two had three kids by then. Different fathers, complicated arrangements, the kind of family tree that required a diagram to explain. She was doing her best, which in our family meant she was surviving, keeping everyone fed, showing up most of the time.

The arrangement made sense on paper. She worked nights - cleaning, I think, or maybe hospitality, one of those jobs that happens while normal people sleep. I'd watch the kids overnight, she'd watch them during the day while I worked whatever job I could find. Tag team parenting. Division of labour.

It worked for about five minutes.

The problem was the nights she didn't come home.

It would start with a text. Running late. Then nothing. No call, no update, no explanation. I'd be stuck with three kids who weren't mine, watching the clock, waiting for someone who wasn't coming.

And I'd have to call in sick to work. Again.

"I can't come in today, something came up." The same excuse, over and over, until the excuses stopped working and the job stopped existing. My pattern of three-month employment continued, only now it wasn't just my fault. Now I had help.

When Aunty Two finally came home - the next morning, sometimes the afternoon - I'd try to talk to her about it. Explain that I needed to work, that I couldn't keep calling in, that this arrangement only functioned if she held up her end.

She never understood what she'd done wrong. Or she understood and didn't care. Or she was so deep in her own chaos that my chaos didn't register. We were two people drowning, taking turns pulling each other under.

Then she met a guy.

This was typical Aunty Two. Men appeared in her life like weather events - sudden, intense, and usually destructive. This one seemed different, she said. This one was serious.

Within a month, he'd moved in. Within another month, he'd proposed. Within another month, they were married.

I watched it happen with the detached fascination of someone observing a nature documentary. This is how my family does relationships. Whirlwind and wreckage. No one dates for a year, gets to know each other, makes careful decisions. We just collide and hope for the best.

The wedding was small. Quick. The kind of ceremony that's more about paperwork than celebration. I was there, standing witness to something I already suspected wouldn't last.

What I remember clearly is what happened after.

A month after the wedding, Aunty Two was pregnant. And then, almost immediately, she wasn't. She'd terminated the pregnancy and gotten her tubes tied. All without telling her husband.

He wanted kids. His own kids, biological children, a family built with this woman he'd just married. And she'd made a unilateral decision to ensure that would never happen - without a conversation, without his input, without any acknowledgment that marriage might involve consulting your partner about major life decisions.

I don't know her reasons. Maybe she knew the marriage was already doomed. Maybe she knew she couldn't handle more children. Maybe she just couldn't face another pregnancy, another birth, another eighteen years of responsibility. I understand the impulse, even if I don't understand the execution.

The relationship was over within weeks of him finding out. He moved out. The whirlwind reversed itself, destruction following creation, everything back to chaos.

Then the father of one of her kids moved back in.

Not the husband. One of the earlier ones. The father of one of her children, someone who'd been in and out of the picture for years. Suddenly he was in again, living in the house, part of the daily routine.

He told me something I've never forgotten.

He'd met up with Aunty Two the day before her wedding. They'd slept together. The day before she married another man, she'd been in bed with her ex.

I don't know why he told me. Maybe he thought I should know. Maybe he was staking a claim, asserting that he'd always been there, that the husband had been an interruption. Maybe he just liked drama.

What I took from it was simpler: Aunty Two was just as messed up as I was.

We were chaos twins. Products of the same broken system, the same dysfunctional family, the same patterns repeating across generations. She wasn't a stable adult who could help me get my life together. She was another version of me, a few years further down the same path, making the same mistakes with higher stakes.

I needed to get out.

I found a sharehouse. Some random arrangement with people I didn't know well, the kind of living situation you end up in when you're young and broke and need somewhere to be. It was better than Aunty Two's chaos, at least. My own space. My own disasters.

And then I met him.

We worked together. Retail - and for once, I'd actually stayed. This was the first job I held for more than three months. A couple of years, actually. Something about it worked, or maybe I was finally learning, or maybe I was just tired of starting over. He was there. I was there. The proximity did what proximity does.

We had sex. I got pregnant.

This seems fast because it was fast. We weren't dating. We weren't in a relationship. We were two people who worked together and hooked up and suddenly faced the consequences of biology.

We moved in together. What else were we going to do? I was pregnant, he was the father, this is what people did. You made a mistake and then you tried to turn the mistake into a life.

He was a good person. I want to be clear about that.

Not perfect, not a saint, but genuinely decent in a way that I wasn't used to. He came from a family that functioned. Parents who were still together, who had stable jobs, who lived in a house they owned. Normal people with normal lives who'd raised a normal son.

He had no idea what he'd gotten into with me.

I was insecure. Constantly. Every interaction was filtered through the certainty that he would leave, that I wasn't good enough, that this was temporary and I needed to prepare for the inevitable abandonment. I couldn't relax into the relationship because relaxing meant trusting, and trusting meant being vulnerable, and being vulnerable meant getting hurt.

I was terrible with money. Still. Always. The spending continued, the debt accumulated, the financial chaos that had followed me since my first job continued to follow me now. We had a baby coming and I couldn't stop buying things we didn't need, couldn't make a budget and stick to it, couldn't be the responsible adult that parenthood required.

And I was scared. Terrified, actually. Of being pregnant, of giving birth, of becoming a mother. I'd seen what mothers in my family looked like. Teenage pregnancies, neglect, abuse, children raised in caravans and chaos. I was certain - absolutely certain - that I would screw this up. That whatever was broken in Nan, in Mum, in all of them, was broken in me too.

The baby came anyway. Biology doesn't wait for you to be ready.

My daughter was born when I was nineteen.

She was perfect. Tiny and loud and completely dependent on me for everything. I looked at her face and felt love and terror in equal measure. This small human needed me to not mess up. The stakes had never been higher.

I discovered childcare almost immediately.

This sounds mercenary, I know. Cold. What kind of mother puts her newborn in childcare and goes back to work? What kind of mother outsources the most important job she'll ever have?

The kind who doesn't trust herself.

Childcare meant professionals. People who'd been trained to look after children, who knew what they were doing, who wouldn't screw up the way I was certain to screw up. If my daughter spent her days with qualified caregivers instead of with me, maybe she'd turn out okay. Maybe she'd escape the damage that I was sure I'd inflict.

It was the safest option. That's how I justified it. I was protecting her - from myself.

I went back to work six weeks after she was born. Put her in childcare. Told myself this was responsible, practical, the right choice. Tried not to think about what it said about my confidence in my own mothering.

The relationship deteriorated.

We were too different. He was stable; I was chaos. He planned for the future; I couldn't see past next week. He wanted a partner; I was barely holding myself together.

And I lied.

This was new - or rather, it was the beginning of a pattern that would define my life. I lied about money. About where it went, what I spent it on, how much debt I was accumulating. I lied to cover the shopping, the gambling that had started creeping in, the financial destruction I was creating.

I wasn't good at it yet. The lies were clumsy, transparent, easily caught. He'd find receipts, notice discrepancies, ask questions I couldn't answer. Each discovery was a crack in whatever trust we'd built.

We got evicted. Couldn't pay rent - my fault, mostly, the money disappearing into my chaos instead of into the landlord's account. We had to move in with his parents.

His parents. The normal ones with the stable house and the functional family. They took in their son, his girlfriend, and their grandchild, and they tried to help. They were kind.

I couldn't receive it. The kindness felt like judgment, even when it wasn't. Their stability highlighted my instability. Their competence showcased my disasters.

Within a couple of weeks, he asked me to leave.

He couldn't keep our daughter. Work commitments, logistics, whatever the practical reasons were. So when I left, she came with me.

My daughter and me. Alone. Heading back to Brisbane because that's where I always ended up, the gravitational centre of my chaos.

I'd had a chance. A decent man, a functional family, a shot at building something different. And I'd burned it down the way I always burned things down - with lies and spending and the self-destruction that I couldn't seem to stop.

He'd remain in her life. Weekend dad, co-parent, the stable presence that I couldn't be. Years later, my daughter would gravitate toward him, toward his normalcy, away from my mess. I don't blame her for that. I pushed for them to have a relationship. I just didn't expect that the relationship would highlight everything I wasn't.

But that was in the future. For now, I was twenty years old, back in Brisbane, single mother, carrying my daughter toward whatever came next.

The pattern was clear, even if I couldn't see it yet.

Get something good. Destroy it. Start over. Repeat.

I just hadn't figured out how to break the cycle.

I was too busy living it.

| 14 |

The First Big Lie

Back in Brisbane. Back in a caravan.

Some things never change. Some patterns are so deep they feel like gravity - no matter how high you jump, you end up back on the ground. For me, the ground was always a caravan park. The temporary housing that kept becoming permanent.

But this time I had my daughter.

She was a toddler now, walking and talking and becoming a person. Watching her navigate the cramped space of the caravan, I felt the full weight of what I'd created. This wasn't just my life anymore. Every choice I made shaped her world too.

The caravan was cheap. That was the point. I didn't have money for a proper rental - not with the debt I'd accumulated, not with my credit history, not with the financial destruction I'd left behind. A caravan was what I could afford, so a caravan was what we got.

It wasn't great. But it was ours.

I got a job. A good one, relatively speaking.

The work itself wasn't glamorous - nothing I've ever done has been glamorous - but it paid well. Better than retail, better than minimum wage, better than anything I'd managed before. For the first time in my life, I was earning enough to actually build something.

And something shifted.

Maybe it was my daughter. Maybe it was hitting some internal rock bottom that I hadn't known existed. Maybe I was just tired - exhausted from the chaos, from the scrambling, from the constant cycle of destruction and starting over.

Whatever it was, I started working. Really working. Showing up on time. Staying the whole shift. Doing what was asked and more. Being reliable.

They say it takes thirty days to build a habit. It took me longer than that. Months of fighting my own impulses, of dragging myself to work when I didn't want to go, of choosing responsibility over comfort. But slowly, painfully, something changed.

I developed a work ethic.

It sounds simple. For most people, it probably is simple - you work because you have to, because that's what adults do, because bills exist and money doesn't appear by magic. But for me, it was a revelation. The discovery that showing up consistently actually led somewhere. That effort accumulated. That I could be someone who was trusted.

I learned to cook.

Another thing that sounds simple. Another thing that wasn't.

No one had taught me. Nan didn't cook. Mum's meals were inconsistent at best. I'd grown up on takeaway and convenience food and whatever was cheapest and easiest. The idea of preparing a meal from ingredients - actually cooking, with recipes and techniques and multiple steps - was foreign.

But I had a daughter. And I didn't want her growing up the way I had, eating pizza every night, never seeing someone put effort into feeding her.

So I taught myself. Badly, at first. Burnt things and undercooked things and combinations that didn't work. But I kept trying. Found recipes I could manage. Built a small repertoire of meals I could make reliably.

It wasn't gourmet. It was just food, prepared by her mother, served at whatever passed for a table in our caravan. But it mattered. It was different from what I'd known.

We went places on weekends.

This seems small, but it wasn't. In my childhood, weekends were just days. Nothing special happened. You existed through them the same way you existed through weekdays.

But I wanted something different for my daughter. I wanted her to have experiences, memories, the sense that life could be more than just survival.

So we went to parks. To playgrounds. To free events and cheap activities, anywhere a toddler could run around and laugh and be a kid. I didn't have money for expensive outings, but I had time, and I had a car that mostly worked, and I had the determination to give her something I'd never had.

Those weekends were good. Simple and good. My daughter and me, building a life that looked nothing like the one I'd grown up in.

I was doing it. Breaking the cycle. Becoming someone different.

And then I found a way to destroy it.

I met some people.

They weren't friends. I know that now. Friends don't lead you toward destruction. Friends don't introduce you to the things that will ruin your life. But at the time, they felt like friends. They felt like excitement, like escape, like proof that I was still young and could still have fun.

There were drugs. Not for me - my body had already taught me it rejected that stuff - but the people around me were always on something. Pills, powders, substances that made them louder and looser and more reckless. I didn't partake, but I was there. I was part of the scene.

There was alcohol. Lots of it. Nights out that turned into mornings, drinking until I couldn't feel the weight of my life pressing down on me.

And there was a way to make money.

Prostitution is a strong word. I didn't stand on street corners or work in brothels. But I figured out that men would pay for my company, and that a few hours of "work" could equal what I made in a week at my regular job. Quick money. Easy money. Money that didn't require showing up on time or being reliable or any of the habits I'd worked so hard to build.

It started small. Occasional. Just something on the side, a way to supplement income, nothing serious.

It became more.

My daughter spent more time with her dad.

He was still in her life - the stable one, the good one, the parent who had his shit together. When I started going out more, staying out later, being less available, he stepped up. Took her on weekends. Kept her extra nights. Did what needed to be done because I wasn't doing it.

I told myself this was fine. Good, even. She was with her father, she was safe, she was better off with him than with me when I was... doing whatever I was doing.

The truth was simpler: I was choosing the party over my child.

Not every time. Not completely. But enough. Enough that she learned her mother wasn't always there. Enough that the weekends at the park became less frequent. Enough that the life I'd been building started to crumble under the weight of my bad decisions.

The old pattern was back. Get something good, destroy it, start over.

I just hadn't finished the destruction yet.

I had a boyfriend during this time. One of the people from the party crowd.

He was part of the scene - drugs, drinking, the whole lifestyle. We weren't good for each other. We weren't good for anyone. But we were together, in whatever way people like us were together.

When I found out I was pregnant, he ran.

Gone. Disappeared. The moment the word "pregnant" entered the conversation, he was out the door and out of my life. No discussion, no responsibility, just gone.

I couldn't even be surprised. This was what men did in my experience. They appeared, they did damage, they vanished. The only unusual thing was the timing - most of them waited until after the crisis to leave.

But here's the thing: I wasn't even sure he was the father.

The lifestyle I'd been living... there had been others. The prostitution, the partying, the blurred nights where I didn't always remember what had happened or with whom. I'd been careless in ways that I'm still ashamed to write down.

I was pregnant, and I didn't know whose baby it was.

The second pregnancy was different from the first.

With my first daughter, I'd had a partner. Someone to share the fear, the responsibility, the planning. It hadn't worked out, but at least I hadn't been alone.

This time I was alone. Completely. The father - whoever he was - wasn't going to step up. The party friends had evaporated the moment things got serious. My family was... my family. No help there.

I thought about my options. Really thought about them. Considered not going through with it, considered adoption, considered every alternative to becoming a single mother of two with no support and no resources.

But I couldn't do it. Whatever was growing inside me was mine, was a person, was happening whether I was ready or not. I'd made the choices that led here. Now I had to live with them.

When my second daughter was born, I had to make a decision.

She would ask, eventually. Every child asks. Where did I come from? Who is my father? What's the story of how I got here?

And I had two options. Tell the truth: I don't know who your father is because I was living a life I'm ashamed of and I was careless and I made terrible choices. Or tell a lie.

I chose the lie.

Your father died before you were born.

That's what I told her. What I've always told her. A simple story, tragic but clean. A father who existed, who would have been there, who was taken away by circumstances beyond anyone's control.

It's not true. I don't know if her father is alive or dead. I don't know who he is. I've never tried to find out, never done the DNA test, never wanted to open that particular door.

The lie was easier. For me, definitely. But I told myself it was easier for her too. Better to have a dead father than a mystery. Better to have a clean story than a complicated one. Better to believe you were wanted by someone who couldn't be there than to wonder if you were wanted at all.

She'll find out eventually.

That's the thing about lies. They hold until they don't. Someday she'll do an ancestry test for fun, or dig into records, or just ask the right questions to the right people. The truth will surface because truth always surfaces.

And when it does, she'll hate me.

I've made peace with that. Or I've tried to. I've accepted that the lie I told to protect her - to protect myself, really, let's be honest - will eventually become the thing that destroys our relationship.

But I couldn't tell her. Not then, not now, not ever. The truth is too ugly. The truth is that her mother was lost in a period of such profound self-destruction that she doesn't know who fathered her child. That's not a story anyone wants to hear about their own origin.

So I lie. The first big lie. The one I've maintained for her entire life.

Your father died before you were born.

I'm sorry.

Six weeks after she was born, I went back to work.

Same pattern as before. Childcare as safety net. Professionals doing what I didn't trust myself to do. Only now there were two children, two sets of fees, two small humans depending on me to keep it together.

I stopped the partying. Mostly. The pregnancy had been a wake-up call, or at least a pause button. I couldn't be that person and be a mother to two children. Something had to give.

So I gave up the worst of it. Pulled back from the crowd, from the lifestyle, from the choices that had led me here. Started over again, the way I always started over.

But the lie stayed with me. The first big lie, foundational, something I'd have to maintain forever or watch everything collapse.

I'd told myself for years that I was a bad liar. Clumsy. Transparent. Easily caught.

Turned out I just needed higher stakes.

When it mattered, I could lie just fine.

| 15 |

The Abuse Without Bruises

I met him at work.

This was becoming a pattern - finding partners in the places I spent my days, letting proximity do the work of connection. After the disaster of the party crowd, after the pregnancy with no father, after pulling myself back together for the hundredth time, I was trying to be normal. Going to work. Coming home. Being a mother.

He seemed normal too. That was the appeal.

We moved in together within a month.

I know how that sounds. I know it's fast, reckless, exactly the kind of whirlwind that had destroyed my Aunty Two's marriage. But I was tired of being alone. Tired of doing everything myself - two kids, a job, a life that felt like it was held together with tape and desperation. He offered partnership. He offered help. He offered someone to share the weight.

I said yes before I knew what I was saying yes to.

Four months later, I was pregnant again.

He wasn't like Stepdad. That's what I told myself at first.

There was no violence. No holes in walls, no cane across knuckles, no head smashed into bed frames. He never hit me. Never raised a hand. If you'd asked me in those early months whether I was in an abusive relationship, I would have laughed. I knew what abuse looked like. I'd grown up with it. This wasn't that.

But abuse doesn't always leave bruises.

It took me years to learn the vocabulary. Gaslighting. Financial abuse. Coercive control. Isolation. Back then, these weren't terms I knew. They weren't things people talked about, at least not in my world. Abuse meant getting hit. Everything else was just... relationships being hard.

So I didn't recognise what was happening. Not at first. Not for a long time.

It started small. It always starts small.

He needed to know where I was. All the time. Not in a caring way - in a monitoring way. Where are you going, when will you be back, who are you with, why didn't you answer your phone immediately? Questions that felt like concern but were actually surveillance.

I adapted. I always adapted. I told him where I was going before I went. I answered my phone on the first ring. I made myself trackable, predictable, because that's what kept the peace.

He wanted me to stay home with the kids. That was the proper thing for a mother to do, he said. Why was I working when I should be raising our children? What kind of mother prioritised a job over her family?

But when I stayed home, the criticism shifted. I wasn't contributing. I was lazy. I was spending his money without earning any of my own. What did I even do all day?

I couldn't win. That was the point. The rules changed depending on what would make me feel worst. Work, and I was a bad mother. Stay home, and I was a lazy freeloader. Either choice was wrong because the goal wasn't for me to make the right choice. The goal was for me to feel perpetually inadequate.

I cooked dinner every night.

I'd learned to cook for my first daughter, taught myself from nothing, built a small collection of meals I could make with confidence. Now cooking became a minefield.

I'd serve dinner and wait for the verdict. Sometimes it was fine. Sometimes it was "this is shit" or "why can't you make anything good" or a heavy sigh that communicated disappointment without words. I never knew which it would be. The same meal could be acceptable one night and terrible the next.

I started dreading dinner. Started second-guessing every ingredient, every technique, every choice. The thing I'd taught myself to do, the skill I'd built from nothing, became a source of anxiety instead of pride.

That's how it works. You take something someone is proud of and you chip away at it until they doubt themselves. Until they need your approval to feel okay. Until they're so busy trying to please you that they forget they ever pleased themselves.

My family disappeared.

Not literally - they were still out there, still existing in their various states of dysfunction. But I stopped seeing them. Stopped calling. Stopped maintaining whatever fragile connections had survived everything else.

He didn't like them. That was the surface reason. They were trashy, embarrassing, not the kind of people he wanted associated with his life. Every visit, every phone call, every mention of my family became an opportunity for criticism.

And he was right, in a way. My family was a mess. Nan, Mum, the aunties - none of them were winning any awards for functional adulthood. It was easy to agree when he pointed out their flaws. Easy to distance myself from the chaos I'd grown up in.

But that was the trap. Each person I cut off was one less person who might notice something was wrong. One less outside perspective. One less escape route.

By the time I realised how isolated I'd become, I had no one left to call.

He didn't like my friends either.

The same pattern. Criticism, disapproval, subtle and not-so-subtle pressure to stop seeing them. They were a bad influence. They didn't like him. They were filling my head with ideas.

Friends notice things. Friends ask questions. Friends say "are you okay?" and "you seem different" and "I'm worried about you." Friends are dangerous when you're trying to control someone.

So the friends went away too. One by one, dropped or driven off, until it was just me and him and the kids in a house that felt increasingly like a prison.

I couldn't have friends. That's what I learned. Friends find out. Friends complicate things. Friends are a liability.

It's a lesson I've carried ever since.

I got a work-from-home job.

This was when technology was changing, when computers were becoming something normal people could use, when new kinds of work were emerging. I taught myself enough to be useful, found a job I could do from home, started earning money again.

He hated it.

Not at first - at first it was fine, acceptable, a way for me to contribute without leaving the house. But the job gave me something he hadn't anticipated: independence. My own income. My own sense of competence. Something that was mine, that he couldn't control.

The criticism intensified. I was always working. I was neglecting the kids, neglecting him, neglecting my responsibilities. The job was making me difficult. The job was giving me ideas.

When my phone rang for work, I answered it. That was the job - being available, being responsive, doing what was required. But every work call became an argument. Why did I answer? Couldn't it wait? Why was I prioritising strangers over my own family?

One day, I answered a work call and something snapped.

Not in him. In me.

I finished the call. Put down the phone. Looked at him standing there, ready to start the usual argument, and I found something I didn't know I still had.

"Pack your shit and get out."

The words came from somewhere deep. Some last reserve of self that hadn't been eroded away. Some tiny piece that remembered I'd existed before him, that I could exist after him.

He didn't believe me at first. We'd had fights before, said things in anger, always smoothed it over. This was just another moment of friction that would pass.

But I meant it. For the first time, I really meant it.

He left. Packed his things and went, stunned that the woman he'd spent years diminishing had suddenly found a spine.

And then I was alone. With three kids. In a house I couldn't afford. With no friends, no family connections, no support system.

The prison door was open. I just had to figure out how to survive on the other side.

What happened next is the hardest part of this story to tell.

We had a son together. A little boy, born into that relationship, connected to both of us. When the relationship ended, there was a question: where would he live?

He went with his father.

I need to sit with this. I need to tell it honestly, even though the honesty burns.

I didn't fight. When the custody question came up, when decisions were being made about where our son would live, I didn't fight for him. I was paralysed. Frozen. So depleted from years of being worn down that I couldn't muster the energy to battle for my own child.

I told people I had no choice. That's the lie I used, the story I told to make it bearable. The system decided. The circumstances dictated. My hands were tied.

But I had a choice. I just didn't make it.

I was so broken, so exhausted, so convinced of my own inadequacy that I let my son go without a fight. I told myself he'd be better off. Told myself I couldn't handle three kids alone. Told myself whatever I needed to tell myself to get through the day.

The truth is simpler and uglier: I failed him.

Twelve years later, my son came home to me.

Twelve years with his father. Twelve years of whatever happened in that house, whatever was done or not done, whatever damage accumulated while I wasn't there to protect him.

He doesn't talk about all of it. I don't push. But I know enough to know that my failure to fight had consequences. That the years he spent away from me weren't easy. That my paralysis had a cost, and he's the one who paid it.

Everything that happened to him is my fault.

I own that. I should have fought. I should have found the strength, found the resources, found whatever it took to keep my child with me. I was his mother. Protecting him was my job. And I failed.

Some things you can't make up for. Some damage you can't undo. You can only acknowledge it, carry it, and try to do better with whatever time is left.

My son is with me now. We're building something, slowly. But those twelve years are a gap that can never be filled. A wound that scarred over but never healed.

After he left, after the custody was decided, after I was alone with my two daughters in a house that felt too big and too quiet, I made another decision.

I was done being a victim.

Done with men who controlled and diminished. Done with relationships that required me to shrink. Done with the pattern that had defined my life since I was old enough to date.

I had two daughters watching me. Learning from me. Absorbing lessons about what women accept, what relationships look like, what they should expect from their own futures.

I couldn't teach them to repeat my mistakes. I had to show them something different.

So I focused on work. The computer skills I'd developed, the job I'd been doing from home - I leaned into it. Built competence. Became valuable. Started to see a path forward that didn't involve depending on anyone else.

The corporate world was out there, somewhere beyond the chaos I'd always known. Normal people with normal jobs and normal lives. People who didn't know about caravans and custody battles and all the ways I'd failed.

Maybe I could become one of them.

Maybe I could become someone else entirely.

The idea was taking shape. The lie was beginning to form.

But first, I had to learn how to be alone without falling apart.

First, I had to figure out who I was without someone else telling me.

| 16 |

The Reinvention

The corporate world was an alien planet.

I'd spent my entire life in the margins - caravans and housing commission, retail jobs and chaos, people who scraped by and called it living. The idea that there was another world out there, one with office buildings and business cards and people who said things like "circle back" and "action items," had always been abstract. Something that happened to other people.

Now I was trying to become one of those other people.

The work-from-home job had taught me computers. I'd picked it up the way I'd picked up everything - necessity as teacher, desperation as motivation. I wasn't an expert, but I knew enough to be useful. And useful, it turned out, could get you through a lot of doors.

I found a job. Entry level, bottom of the ladder, the kind of position they give to people who don't have degrees or connections but seem willing to learn. Monday to Friday. Regular hours. An office with fluorescent lights and a break room with a coffee machine that everyone complained about but no one fixed.

It fit with the kids. School hours, mostly. Childcare filled the gaps. For the first time in my life, I had a schedule that looked like what normal people had.

I just had to figure out how to be a normal person.

The first rule I learned was: keep your mouth shut.

Not permanently. Not about work things. But about myself, about my past, about anything that might reveal where I'd come from.

I listened instead. Sat in meetings and break rooms and casual conversations, absorbing how these people talked, what they talked about, the references and assumptions that shaped their world.

They talked about holidays. Overseas trips, beach houses, ski seasons. They talked about their kids' private schools and their renovations and their investment properties. They talked about wine regions and restaurants and suburbs I'd never heard of.

They talked about their families. Parents who'd paid for university. Siblings who were lawyers, doctors, accountants. Childhoods that sounded like something from a television show - stable, supported, unremarkable in their functionality.

And they talked about bogans.

The first time I heard it, I was in the break room.

A group of colleagues, mid-conversation, laughing about something. I was making tea, half-listening, trying to seem casual.

"...absolute bogan, you should have seen the car. Rusted out Commodore with a southern cross sticker..."

Laughter. Agreement. Someone else chiming in.

"That whole area's like that. Housing commission central. You couldn't pay me to live there."

More laughter. The easy, unconscious cruelty of people who've never had to worry about where they'd live.

They named the suburb. The actual suburb, specific and unmistakable.

The suburb I grew up in.

I stood very still. Kept my face neutral. Finished making my tea. Walked back to my desk without saying anything.

My hands were shaking.

It happened again. And again.

Bogan jokes were currency in that office. A way of bonding, of establishing who was in and who was out. We're not like those people. We worked hard. We made good choices. We belong here and they belong there, in their housing commission houses with their rusted cars and their dysfunction.

I laughed along.

What else could I do? Say "actually, I grew up there"? Watch their faces change, watch them recategorise me, watch everything I was trying to build collapse because of where I'd started?

So I laughed. Agreed. Participated in the mockery of people exactly like my family, exactly like the people I'd grown up with, exactly like who I'd been before I walked through the door of this office.

Each laugh was a small erasure. A deletion of my own history. A choice to be one of them instead of one of us.

The questions started coming.

Small talk. Getting-to-know-you conversations. The normal social rituals of a workplace.

Where did you grow up? What school did you go to? What do your parents do? Do you have siblings?

Simple questions. The kind that people with normal backgrounds answer without thinking.

For me, each one was a landmine.

I couldn't say the truth. The suburb I grew up in was a punchline. My schooling was fragmented and unremarkable. My parents - which ones? The teenage mother who kicked me out? The stepfather who put her head through walls? The grandmother who smashed my head into a bed frame? My siblings were half-siblings scattered across states, most of whom I barely knew.

The truth was unspeakable. So I started speaking something else.

I invented a childhood.

It happened gradually, not all at once. A question here, a detail there, building a story that was nothing like my actual life.

I grew up in a different suburb. A respectable one, the kind that didn't make people laugh or look away. I picked it almost randomly - somewhere I'd driven through once or twice, somewhere plausible but not traceable.

I went to a particular school. A real school, one that existed, one that I researched just enough to answer basic questions. I joined in year ten, I said, explaining why I wouldn't know anyone from the earlier years. My family moved a lot.

My parents were strict. Religious. That explained everything - why I didn't drink much, why I didn't talk about family, why I seemed reserved about my past. Religious upbringing was a door-closer. People nodded and moved on, not wanting to pry into someone's faith.

I was an only child. Simpler that way. No siblings to explain, no complicated family tree, no half-relationships to navigate.

The lie was clean. Compact. Consistent.

I practised it in front of mirrors. Told it until it felt natural, until the hesitation disappeared, until I could answer questions about my fictional childhood without my voice wavering.

I became someone else.

The strange thing was how easy it was.

I'd thought lying would be hard. That I'd slip up, contradict myself, get caught in the web of my own making. That someone would ask a question I couldn't answer and the whole thing would collapse.

But no one checks. That's the secret. No one calls your high school to verify you went there. No one drives to the suburb you claim to be from and asks if anyone remembers you. No one does the work of investigating a colleague's background story.

They just accept what you tell them. Why wouldn't they? Who lies about where they grew up?

People like me. That's who.

I listened more than I talked. That was the key.

When you're building a fake identity, the less you say, the less you can get wrong. So I asked questions instead. Drew people out about their lives, their families, their experiences. Seemed interested - and sometimes actually was interested - in who they were and where they came from.

This made me seem like a good listener. A thoughtful colleague. Someone who cared about others rather than just talking about themselves.

Really, I was gathering data. Learning how normal people talked about their lives so I could mimic it. Studying the rhythms and references of middle-class existence so I could perform it convincingly.

Every conversation was research. Every interaction was practice.

I was building a character, and the office was my stage.

The performance extended beyond backstory.

I watched how people dressed and adjusted my wardrobe. Listened to how they spoke and moderated my accent, my vocabulary, the slang that would mark me as from somewhere else. Noticed what they knew and didn't know, what references landed and which ones fell flat.

I became a student of normalcy. An anthropologist of the middle class. I observed and imitated until the imitation became habit, until I couldn't always remember which parts were performance and which parts were me.

The accent shifted first. Queensland bogan has a particular sound - vowels that stretch, consonants that blur, a cadence that marks you as clearly as a postcode. I smoothed it out. Listened to how my colleagues spoke and matched them, syllable by syllable, until my voice didn't betray my origins.

The clothes came next. I didn't have money for expensive things, but I learned what looked right. Thrift stores in nice suburbs had cast-offs from people who could afford to discard quality. I dressed above my pay grade, invested in looking like I belonged.

The knowledge took longer. There were gaps - things everyone seemed to know that I'd never learned. Cultural references, historical facts, the baseline education that came from stable schooling and engaged parents. I read voraciously, watched documentaries, filled in the holes that my chaotic childhood had left.

Slowly, piece by piece, I constructed someone new.

It worked.

That's the thing. The lie worked.

I got promoted. Then promoted again. People respected me, trusted me, assumed I was one of them. The fictional childhood I'd invented became the foundation for a real career, a real reputation, a real life that looked nothing like where I'd started.

Every year the lie got easier. Every year the past got further away. Every year I became more the person I was pretending to be and less the person I'd been born as.

The kid from the caravan park was disappearing. In her place was someone with a respectable suburb and a religious upbringing and a story that didn't make people uncomfortable.

I was winning. Finally, after everything, I was winning.

But winning came with costs.

I couldn't relax. Ever. Every conversation was a potential trap. Every new colleague was someone who might ask the wrong question, know someone from my fake school, trip me up somehow.

I couldn't have close friends. Friends wanted to know you, really know you. They wanted to meet your family, hear your stories, understand your history. I couldn't give them any of that without the lie collapsing.

I couldn't go home. Not to the suburb I'd grown up in, not to the family I'd come from. Any connection to my real past was a thread that could unravel everything.

I was successful and isolated. Respected and alone. The career was real but the person having it was fiction.

This was the trade I'd made. This was the price of reinvention.

I told myself it was worth it. Most days, I believed it.

Fifteen years now. Fifteen years of the lie.

Different jobs, different cities, different stages of life - but always the same story. The respectable suburb. The religious parents. The childhood that explained everything without revealing anything.

The lie has become load-bearing. Pull it out now and everything collapses. The career, the reputation, the life I've built - all of it rests on a foundation of fiction.

Sometimes I wonder who I'd be if I'd told the truth. If I'd walked into that first corporate job and said "I grew up in housing commission, my mum was fifteen when she had me, I've been in and out of foster care and caravans my whole life." Would they have given me a chance? Would I have climbed the ladder, earned the respect, built what I've built?

I don't think so. I think the truth would have disqualified me before I started. I think the bogan jokes would have been about me instead of near me. I think I would have been sorted into a box and left there.

The lie was survival. The lie was the only path from there to here.

But it's also a prison. A very comfortable prison, with a nice house and a pool and a career that pays well. But a prison nonetheless.

I can never stop performing. I can never let the mask slip. I can never be fully known by anyone, because being known would mean being revealed.

This is what breaking the cycle looks like, apparently.

Not clean. Not triumphant. Just a different kind of trap.

But at least it's mine.

| 17 |

Mr Three

I met him at work.

By now I was established. Years into the lie, comfortable in my corporate skin, respected and reliable and completely fictional. I'd climbed the ladder far enough that I had an office instead of a desk, a title that meant something, a salary that would have seemed like fantasy to the girl in the caravan park.

He was a colleague. Smart, successful, from exactly the kind of background I was pretending to have. Good family, good education, good everything. The kind of man who'd never had to reinvent himself because his original version was already acceptable.

We started dating. Carefully, at first - office relationships have rules - but then seriously. Moving toward something real. Something that might last.

And that's when the lie became a problem.

Dating casually is easy when you're living a fiction. Dinner, drinks, surface conversation. You can perform for a few hours, go home, drop the mask, breathe.

But relationships want more. They want depth. They want history and family and all the context that makes a person who they are.

He wanted to meet my family.

This is normal. This is what people in relationships do - introduce each other to parents, to siblings, to the network of people who shaped them. It's a ritual, a milestone, a sign that things are serious.

For me, it was a crisis.

My family couldn't meet him. Not because they'd embarrass me - though they would - but because they'd expose me. One conversation with Nan or Mum or any of my aunties and the whole fiction would collapse. They'd reference the real suburb, the real schools, the real chaos. They'd tell stories that contradicted everything I'd built.

My family was a loaded gun pointed at my carefully constructed life.

So I made sure he never got near them.

The strategy was simple: create distance.

I started picking fights. Called Mum and manufactured an argument about something that didn't matter. Told Nan off for some invented slight. Created conflict where none existed, giving myself a reason to be estranged.

"We're not speaking right now," I'd tell him when he asked about family. "There's some drama. I don't want to get into it."

He accepted this. People have complicated families. It wasn't strange that mine had issues, that I wasn't close to them, that meetings would have to wait until things settled down.

Things never settled down. I made sure of it.

Every few months, I'd manufacture a new conflict. Keep the estrangement fresh. Give myself an ongoing excuse for why he couldn't meet the people I came from.

It was exhausting. Maintaining fake fights on top of a fake identity, managing two separate deceptions at once. But it worked. Year after year, he stayed away from my family because my family and I were "having problems."

The problems were fictional. But they served their purpose.

Friends were the same issue.

He had friends. Lots of them. Good people from his good life, people he'd known since school, people who formed the fabric of his social existence. He wanted to introduce me. He wanted me to become part of his world.

I did, carefully. Met his friends, charmed them, became the person they expected - the woman with the respectable background and the successful career, perfect for their perfect friend.

But integration goes both ways. If I was meeting his friends, shouldn't he meet mine?

I didn't have any.

This is the thing about living a lie: friends find out. Friends ask questions, notice inconsistencies, remember things you said that contradict things you're saying now. Friends are witnesses to your life, and I couldn't afford witnesses.

So I'd kept my social world shallow. Colleagues I was friendly with but not close to. Acquaintances who knew the performance but not the performer. No one who knew me well enough to catch me in a contradiction.

When he asked about my friends, I made excuses. I was private. I'd moved around a lot. I'd lost touch with people over the years. I was close with colleagues, but those were his colleagues too, so that didn't count.

He found this odd. I could tell. But odd isn't the same as suspicious. He filed it under "she's just different" and let it go.

For a while.

Five years is a long time to maintain a performance.

At first, it wasn't hard. The lie was second nature by then. I could recite my fake childhood in my sleep, navigate questions without hesitation, be the person I'd invented without conscious effort.

But relationships deepen. Intimacy grows. The longer you're with someone, the more they see of you - the cracks, the inconsistencies, the moments when the mask slips.

He started asking questions.

Not accusations. Just... curiosity. Wondering about the gaps.

Why didn't I have any photos from my childhood? (Because my childhood wasn't photographed. Because no one cared enough to document it.)

Why didn't I ever talk about my parents with any warmth? (Because my "parents" were fictional constructs I'd invented for convenience.)

Why did my stories about growing up feel rehearsed? (Because they were rehearsed. Because I'd practised them in front of mirrors.)

I had answers for everything. But the answers were starting to feel thin.

We'd argue about my family.

He couldn't understand why, after five years, he still hadn't met a single person I was related to. The ongoing "drama" that kept us apart was starting to seem less like bad luck and more like avoidance.

"What are you hiding?" he asked once.

I deflected. Got angry. Turned it into a fight about trust, about him not respecting my boundaries, about how my family situation was complicated and he needed to accept that.

It worked that time. And the next time. But each argument cost something. Each deflection created distance. Each lie I told to protect the bigger lie eroded whatever we were building.

He wasn't stupid. He knew something was wrong. He just didn't know what.

The questions got harder.

He wanted to know why my oldest daughter was estranged. (Because she'd figured out I was a mess, and she'd chosen her stable father over her chaotic mother.)

He wanted to know why I never visited the suburb I claimed to be from. (Because I'd never actually lived there. Because driving through would reveal how little I knew about the place I supposedly grew up.)

He wanted to know why my life before him seemed to exist only in stories, never in photos or mementos or contact with anyone who'd known me then.

I was running out of explanations. The fiction I'd built was comprehensive, but it wasn't infinitely detailed. There were edges, boundaries, places where the invented history just... stopped.

He was bumping into those boundaries more and more.

Living with someone makes hiding harder.

Little things. The way I flinched at unexpected sounds - a legacy of growing up in houses where loud noises meant violence. The nightmares I couldn't explain, about things that hadn't happened to the person I was pretending to be. The gaps in knowledge that someone with my supposed education should have had.

I'd wake up from a dream, panicked, and he'd ask what was wrong. What could I say? I dreamed about my grandmother smashing my head into a bed frame? I dreamed about being kicked out at fifteen? I dreamed about caravans and housing commission and all the things that never happened to the woman he thought he loved?

I said I didn't remember my dreams. Another lie, layered on top of all the others.

The end came quietly.

No dramatic revelation. No caught-out moment where the whole fiction collapsed. Just a slow accumulation of doubt, distance, disconnection.

We argued more. About my family, about my secrecy, about the walls I kept up no matter how close he tried to get. He wanted all of me, and I could only give him the invented parts.

I could feel him pulling away. Feel him realising that whatever he thought we had wasn't quite real. That the woman he loved was somehow incomplete, unknowable, unreachable.

After five years, I left.

Not because he'd discovered the lie. Because I couldn't maintain it anymore. Because the effort of performing intimacy while hiding my entire history was destroying me. Because I was so tired - tired of watching my words, tired of manufacturing conflicts, tired of being half a person in a relationship that wanted all of me.

I found an executive home. Nice neighbourhood, pool, all the markers of success. Moved in with my two younger kids - my second daughter and my son, who'd finally come home to me. Started over, again, the way I always started over.

The relationship was over, but the lie continued. Had to continue. There was no going back now.

He still doesn't know.

If he reads this book - if anyone who knew me then reads this book - they might put it together. The timeline, the details, the story that sounds familiar if you were there.

I don't know what he'd think. Betrayed, probably. Angry that five years were built on a foundation of fiction. Sad that the woman he thought he knew never actually existed.

Maybe he'd understand. Maybe he'd see why the lie was necessary, why I couldn't have told him the truth, why revealing where I came from would have destroyed everything before it started.

Probably not. The lie is too big. The deception is too fundamental. Understanding has limits.

I think about those five years sometimes.

They were good years, mostly. As good as years can be when you're performing every day, hiding the biggest parts of yourself, building a relationship on a foundation of sand.

He was a good man. Decent. The kind of person who deserved honesty and got fiction instead.

I don't regret the lie - I couldn't have had any of it without the lie. But I regret that the lie made real intimacy impossible. That I could never be fully known. That every moment of closeness was also a moment of concealment.

This is what I gave up for the life I've built. The possibility of being truly seen by another person. The experience of being loved for who you actually are, not who you're pretending to be.

It's a trade-off. Everything is a trade-off.

I chose the lie. I chose the career and the house and the respect. I chose safety over intimacy, success over connection.

Some days that feels like winning.

Other days it feels like the loneliest kind of loss.

After Mr Three, I stopped trying.

Not consciously. I didn't make a decision to be alone forever. But I stopped seeking. Stopped opening doors. Stopped imagining that a relationship could work when I was bringing so much fiction to the table.

It was easier to be alone. Easier to maintain the lie when there was no one in my life asking questions, noticing inconsistencies, wanting to meet the family I couldn't introduce.

The house with the pool is big enough for me and my kids. But in the ways that matter - the adult connection, the partnership, the being truly known - I'm alone. A fortress of success with no one inside who knows the real me.

This is what winning looks like.

This is what I chose.

| 18 |

The Daughter Who Made It

My eldest daughter went to university.

I need to sit with that sentence. Let it sink in. Because in the history of my family - generations of teenage pregnancies, caravans, housing commission, cycles that never broke - no one had ever done that. No one had finished high school and kept going. No one had walked onto a university campus as a student, with a future that required a degree.

She did.

She studied psychology. Of course she did. The daughter of a woman who'd spent her whole life running from her own mind chose to study how minds work. I don't know if that was conscious - an attempt to understand what had happened to her, to me, to all of us - or just where her interests led.

Either way, she finished. Got the degree. First in our family to do it.

She works with kids now. Helping them. Using what she learned to make things better for children who probably remind her of who she used to be.

I should be proud. I am proud, somewhere underneath everything else. But pride isn't the only thing I feel when I think about her.

There's guilt. And anger. And a distance I don't know how to close.

I thought I'd hidden it from her.

The chaos, the dysfunction, all the things I was trying to outrun. I thought if I just kept moving forward, kept building something better, she wouldn't see the mess underneath.

Kids see everything.

She saw me with the bad boyfriends. Saw the moves, the instability, the relationships that started fast and ended badly. She saw her mother struggle and fail and pick herself up and fail again.

She saw me choose men over her. Not consciously, not intentionally, but in the thousand small ways that a mother's romantic disasters pull focus from her children. Every argument I had with a partner was an argument she overheard. Every crisis was a crisis she lived through.

I didn't hide anything. I just told myself I had.

Her father was the stable one.

The first one. The decent man I'd driven away with my lies and my spending and my inability to receive what he offered. He stayed in her life after I left, became the weekend dad, the reliable presence, the parent who had his shit together.

I pushed for that. I want credit for that, at least. I encouraged their relationship, made sure she spent time with him, didn't try to poison her against him the way some mothers do. I knew he was good for her. I knew she needed something I couldn't provide.

But there's a cost to being the chaos parent. The one whose house is unpredictable, whose life is a series of upheavals, whose love comes wrapped in dysfunction.

She gravitated toward him. Naturally. Inevitably. The stable parent is always more appealing than the unstable one. I can't blame her for that.

But it still hurt.

When she was growing up, I was just trying to survive.

That's not an excuse. It's just the truth. I was young - nineteen when I had her - and I had no idea what I was doing. No model for good parenting, no support system, no resources beyond what I could scrape together.

She got childcare instead of a present mother. She got my fear of screwing her up, which probably screwed her up in different ways. She got a mother who was so convinced of her own inadequacy that she outsourced care to professionals rather than trust herself.

I was protecting her. That's what I told myself. Protecting her from me.

Maybe I was. Or maybe I was protecting myself from the vulnerability of really trying. From the possibility of failing at something that mattered.

Either way, she grew up with a mother who was there but not there. Present but distracted. Loving her but also always managing some crisis, some relationship, some disaster that demanded attention.

She deserved better. She got what I could give.

Her dad and I used to have moments.

When she was young, before everything calcified into its current form. We'd co-parent, hand her off, make jokes sometimes. We were never going to be together, but we could be civil. Friendly, even.

She was part of those moments. Watching her parents get along, seeing us laugh at something, experiencing the brief illusion of a functional family.

But there was an edge to it. Times when they'd make fun of me - gentle teasing, nothing cruel, but teasing nonetheless. Times when I was grumpy or stressed or just worn down by life, and they'd share a look. The reasonable parent and the reasonable daughter, tolerating the difficult one.

I felt it. I always felt it. The sense that I was the problem, the outsider, the one who didn't quite fit into the easy dynamic they'd built.

Maybe I was being paranoid. Maybe I was projecting my own insecurities onto innocent moments. But the feeling was real, and it built up over the years like sediment.

When she got older, she chose him.

Not officially. There was no dramatic moment where she announced she was done with me. It was gradual - fewer calls, shorter visits, more distance. The orbit of her life shifted away from me and toward her father, toward his stability, toward the version of family that didn't come with complications.

I don't blame her. I've said that already. I'll keep saying it because I need to believe it.

But I'm also angry.

I pushed for them to have a relationship. For years, I was the one encouraging connection, making sure she saw him, building the bridge between them. I did that because I thought it was right, because I knew she needed him, because I wanted to be the kind of mother who put her child's needs above her own petty feelings.

And now she's on his side of the bridge, and I'm on mine, and the distance between us grows every year.

He didn't return the favour. When she started pulling away from me, he didn't encourage her to maintain the relationship. Didn't say "your mother loves you, you should call her." He just... accepted her choice. Let her drift toward him without pushing her back toward me.

Maybe that's fair. Maybe it's not his job to maintain my relationship with my own daughter. Maybe I'm looking for someone to blame because the alternative is accepting that I drove her away myself.

The guilt is constant.

Every time I think about her, it's there. The knowledge that I wasn't the mother she needed. The awareness of every way I fell short, every choice I made that put something else before her, every moment when I was too broken to give her what she deserved.

She's successful now. Happy, as far as I can tell. Building a life that looks nothing like the one she came from. The cycle is broken, at least for her.

I should take some credit for that. I kept her alive, kept her fed, kept her in schools and childcare where she learned things I couldn't teach her. I didn't hit her, didn't smash her head into bed frames, didn't kick her out at fifteen. The bar was low, and I cleared it.

But clearing a low bar isn't the same as being a good mother. And the guilt knows the difference.

We don't talk much now.

I could pursue it. Call more often, push for visits, refuse to let the distance grow. Some mothers would. Some mothers would fight for the relationship, insist on connection, force their way back into their children's lives.

I don't.

Partly because I'm not sure I have the right. Partly because rejection hurts, and every unreturned call is a small rejection. Partly because I'm tired - tired of fighting, tired of trying, tired of being the one who reaches out only to be met with politeness instead of warmth.

And partly because I feel guilty. The guilt makes me feel like I deserve the distance. Like this is the natural consequence of my failures, and fighting against it would be fighting against justice.

So I let her drift. I let the relationship fade. I tell myself that she knows where to find me if she wants me, and I try not to think about how that's probably what my own mother told herself about me.

The cycle breaks, and then it doesn't. The patterns change, and then they repeat in different forms.

She's the proof that it was worth it.

All of it - the struggle, the lying, the reinvention. She got out. Not because I showed her how, but because I showed her what she didn't want to become. She looked at my life and decided to build something different.

That's a kind of success, I suppose. Not the kind you put in a Christmas card. Not the kind that makes you feel good about yourself. But success nonetheless.

My daughter went to university. My daughter has a career helping kids. My daughter broke the cycle.

She just did it by walking away from me.

If she reads this book, I don't know what she'll think.

Maybe she'll finally understand. See the full picture of what I was dealing with, what I was running from, why I made the choices I made. Maybe context will create compassion.

Or maybe she'll see it as more excuses. More justification for failures that can't be justified. More words from a mother who was always better at explaining herself than being present.

Either way, I want her to know: I'm proud of you.

I'm proud of the woman you became, even though I can't take credit for it. I'm proud of your degree, your career, your life. I'm proud that you chose better than I did, that you built something real, that you broke the cycle even if breaking it meant breaking away from me, Or doing it in spite of me.

I love you. I've always loved you. Even when I was failing you, even when I was choosing wrong, even when I was too broken to show it properly.

I love you.

I'm sorry.

I hope someday that's enough.

| 19 |

Still Lying

It's morning again.

I'm standing in my kitchen, waiting for the coffee machine, looking out at the pool. The skimmer is doing its quiet work. The lawn is neat. The house is everything I ever wanted when I was a kid pressing my face to the window of a caravan, dreaming of something better.

I got it. The something better. The executive home in the nice suburb with the matte black appliances and the stone benchtops. The career that pays well, the title that commands respect, the life that looks exactly like success.

And I'm still lying.

The lie is fifteen years old now. Older than some of my colleagues' children. It's been with me longer than any relationship, longer than most jobs, longer than I've lived in any single place.

I've told it so many times that sometimes I forget it's a lie. I'll be mid-conversation, recounting some detail of my fictional childhood, and for a moment it feels real. The religious parents, the respectable suburb, the stable upbringing - they've become more familiar than my actual memories. The lie has colonised my past.

But then something will trigger it. A news story about foster care. A colleague's joke about bogans. Driving past a caravan park. And the real memories surface, sharp and unwelcome, reminding me who I actually am underneath the performance.

The girl from the caravan park. Nan's charge. Mum's inconvenience. The child nobody wanted enough to fight for.

She's still in here. She never left.

I think about what I've broken to get here.

Family - what's left of it. Nan, cut off years ago when her nastiness became unbearable. Aunty One, who tried to save me and got rejection in return - she looks at me like trash now, and I can't blame her. Aunty Two, still in the cycle, still making the same mistakes. My siblings in Victoria, strangers connected by blood and nothing else. Mum, alive somewhere, unforgiven.

I chose this isolation. Told myself it was necessary, that maintaining the lie required distance, that you can't have a fictional past and a real family who remembers the truth. Every relationship I severed was a thread that might have unravelled everything.

But the cost is real. Holidays alone. No one to call when things go wrong. No shared history with anyone who knew me before I became this.

The lie requires loneliness. I accepted the terms.

I think about my children.

My eldest daughter, who made it out, who broke the cycle by walking away from me. We don't talk much. The distance hurts, but I understand it. She's protecting herself from the chaos I represented. I'd probably do the same.

My second daughter, who carries a lie of her own - the dead father who isn't dead, just unknown. Someday she'll find out. Someday that bomb will explode. I've made my peace with it, or tried to. Some lies have expiration dates. This one is ticking.

My son, who came home after twelve years, who I failed in the most fundamental way a mother can fail. We're building something now, slowly. It's not enough to make up for what I didn't do. Nothing will ever be enough. But it's what I have.

I broke some of the cycle. Not all of it. My kids didn't grow up in caravans. They weren't beaten, weren't abandoned to the system, weren't shuffled between relatives who didn't want them. They had more than I had.

But they also had a mother who was broken in ways she couldn't hide, no matter how hard she tried. They inherited something - not the poverty, not the caravans, but something. The damage finds a way through.

I think about what I've built.

The career is real. The respect is real. The money in my account, the roof over my head, the stability I've created - all real. I earned it. Not through the lie itself, but through the work the lie allowed me to do. The lie got me in the door. What I did after that was mine.

I'm good at my job. I've helped people, built things, contributed something that matters. The person I invented turned out to be capable, competent, valuable. Maybe she was in there all along, buried under the chaos, waiting for a chance to emerge.

Or maybe I created her from nothing. Built her piece by piece, skill by skill, until she became real enough to function. A self-made woman in the most literal sense - I made the self.

I think about the future.

The lie can't last forever. That's the mathematics of it. The more people I meet, the more years that pass, the more chances for someone to connect dots, to recognise a detail, to figure out that the woman with the respectable backstory is actually someone else entirely.

Maybe it will be this book. Someone will read it and think "that sounds familiar" and do the math and realise. Maybe they'll keep my secret. Maybe they won't.

Maybe it will be my daughter's DNA test. Maybe it will be a chance encounter with someone from the old neighbourhood. Maybe it will be something I can't predict, some collision of past and present that finally brings the whole thing down.

I've accepted this. The lie has an expiration date too. I just don't know when.

I started this book by saying I'm a liar.

I'm ending it the same way.

I'm a liar. I've lied about my past, my family, my childhood. I've maintained a fiction for fifteen years and I'll maintain it until I can't anymore. I'm not sorry for the lie. It was survival. It was the only path from there to here.

But I'm also more than a liar.

I'm someone who survived things that should have destroyed me. Who built a life from less than nothing. Who broke enough of the cycle that my kids have a chance, even if I couldn't break all of it. Who found a way to succeed in a world that wasn't designed for people like me.

I'm a liar, and I'm a survivor, and I'm a mother, and I'm a fraud, and I'm a success. All of it, at once, all the time.

That's the truth I can't tell anyone in my real life. The truth that only exists here, in these pages, under a name that isn't mine.

It's still morning. The coffee is ready. The day is waiting.

I'll put on the clothes that match the life I've built. I'll drive the car that doesn't rust. I'll walk into my job and be the person everyone expects - competent, professional, respectable.

No one will know about the caravan park. No one will know about Nan, about Mum, about any of it.

No one will know I'm a liar.

Except you, now. You know.

Thank you for listening. Thank you for letting me tell the truth, just this once, to someone.

And thank you, in advance, for keeping my secret.

I need the lie a little longer.

Maybe forever.

The names in this book have been changed. The places have been obscured. The timeline has been adjusted. But the story is true. Every caravan, every housing commission house, every failure and every small victory - all of it happened. All of it is mine.

I'm still here. Still lying. Still surviving.

That's going to have to be enough.

www.ingramcontent.com/pod-product-compliance
Lightning Source LLC
Chambersburg PA
CBHW071246070526
44583CB00017B/2353